Curriculum of Love

CULTIVATING THE SPIRITUAL NATURE OF CHILDREN

Curriculum of Love

CULTIVATING THE SPIRITUAL NATURE OF CHILDREN

By Morgan Simone Daleo

Illustrated by Frank Riccio

GR∧CE

Grace Publishing & Communications • Charlottesville, Virginia

Curriculum of Love
Cultivating the Spiritual Nature of Children

Grace Publishing & Communications
Charlottesville, VA

Book design by Markus Frey

Printed in Canada on recycled paper.

10 9 8 7 6 5 4 3 2 1

Cataloging in Publication Data

Daleo, Morgan Simone.
    Curriculum of love: cultivating the spiritual nature of children/by Morgan Simone Daleo.
    p. cm.
    Includes bibliographical references.
    ISBN 0-9648799-4-8

Summary: Fostering spiritual development in children through the creative and contemplative arts.

1. Religious education of children. 2. Moral education. 3. Education – Parent participation.
4. Family – Religious life. 5. Children – Religious life. 6. Home schooling. 7. Spiritual exercises.
I. Title.

BL42.D34 1996   291.4'4

For my teachers,
seen and unseen,
especially Avalon Jonah
and Tara Joy.

Acknowledgments

My commitment to the creative arts as a way of working with children is the result of many extraordinary people who have guided me along the journey. Special thanks to Judy Dworin who opened the door to movement and the creative process as pathways of joy for all people, to Mara Capy whose love of movement and stories will live forever, to Irmgard Bartenieff, Deborah Hay and Zuleikha for helping me experience the body as an instrument of Spirit, and to Rob Kaplan and Allaudin Mathieu for opening my ears to the profound joy in making and listening to sound.

My appreciation to Stephen Minot, for sharing the craft of writing, and teaching me to value editing and revision.

I am grateful to the many people who directly contributed to the making of this book, especially Lauren Kaufmann and Alison Stavchansky for their editing skills and generous support. Thanks to Deb Werksman for helpful comments on the manuscript early on in the process. I thank Kathryn Williams for her work on bibliographical annotations and Anne Colony for proofreading.

My thanks to Ellen Duffy, Head of Children and Youth Services at Jefferson - Madison Regional Library in Charlottesville, and to Mary Gordon Hall, singer and radio host at WTJU, Charlottesville for their help with music listings.

Heartfelt thanks to Robin Casarjian, Roxanne Daleo, Ingrid Jones and Barbara Leger for supporting this work.

I would also like to acknowledge my family, and my first teachers, Anne and Michael Daleo, whose intuitive curriculum has always been love.

Table of Contents

Introduction

This book is written for parents, teachers and caregivers who, like myself, try to provide an atmosphere of love and respect in which children's true spiritual nature can grow freely.

Our children are, as indeed we all are, children of God, spiritual beings living in what appears as a physical world. Thus the education we require to develop as truly compassionate and intelligent human beings needs a curriculum which honors our true nature, celebrates the great gift of life and recognizes the importance of taking care of ourselves, our human and animal families and the world we inhabit.

The lessons in this curriculum grew out of developing a homeschool course of study for my son, Avalon. I asked myself, "What does my son need to learn?" I wasn't satisfied with maintaining a merely academic pursuit of learning, nor was I content to allow him to discover his own areas of interest without any guidance on my part. I wanted to provide a learning experience rooted in my own sense of values, reflecting the sacredness of our human experience.

Perhaps too, my quest was piqued by a visit to a public school cafeteria at lunch time, where I watched hundreds of young children rushing through the motions of getting, consuming and throwing away food without a sense of gratitude, respect or thoughtfulness. I returned home determined to create a guide to cultivating values in any environment where children study, learn and play.

I received the ideas for a *Curriculum of Love* through prayer and contemplation. Although I was raised Roman Catholic, I have spent much of my adult life pursuing both Western and Eastern spiritual traditions in order to understand the principles of the world's religions which connect us to God and one another, rather than separate us in the name of belief. I have longed for a way to talk about spiritual values without dogma or strict definitions. My hope is to understand the basic truths which help us to be loving, peaceful and useful human beings.

Though my personal search has led me back to the roots of my Christian tradition, I believe lessons such as being of service, celebrating community and creating joy are truly non-denominational, and applicable to anyone seeking a means of opening the doorway to their child's spiritual understanding of the world.

This book is designed to accommodate the language and beliefs of those who use it. If you find the curriculum lacking in a specific religious orientation which you feel is vital, then utilize that language when presenting the material. If you find the language and concepts presented here to be too limited, or too general, then by all means use your own language of spirit to express the ideas suggested. This is especially true for the words you use to describe the Divine Mystery, Limitless Source, Great Spirit, God.

Parenting and the teaching of children is a challenging path of unknown turns and unexpected surprises. After nearly twenty years of teaching, and nine years of mothering, I have come to see the challenges not as obstacles to my spiritual development, but as pathways of growth, love, forgiveness and faith.

Our children are indeed our teachers. They mirror back to us our behavior, perceptions and beliefs. As teachers, parents and caregivers, we cannot be complacent in leaving the education of our young and inherently wise children to academic and political agendas. If we do, we may be leaving out the essence, the very heart of what is important for our children's welfare, and for our future: the understanding of ourselves as loving human beings.

How to Use This Book

This book is not meant as a step-by-step recipe for spirituality, but rather as a resource of ideas designed to stimulate the growth of compassionate, caring human beings.

I have purposefully left the definition of spirituality open. I've also chosen not to root this curriculum in any one particular doctrine, or religious affiliation. I strongly believe it is our task to follow the inner yearning for truth, for wisdom, for meaning in our lives, and to encourage our children to do the same. This is a book about possible ways to approach spirituality.

In doing so, there are some questions which arise. How does this curriculum fit in with a child's traditional religious education? How do we arrive at a common language of spirit if our beliefs diverge?

I have tried to make this curriculum practical. It is designed as a collection of activities centered on ten core values: harmony, mindfulness, service, self-reliance, community, history (the human adventure), compassion, beauty, balance and joy. These lessons form a curriculum of love, designed to help adults creatively encourage a caring attitude in children.

This curriculum is not meant to be a substitute for a family's own religious education, nor to provide a philosophy of spirituality. It is given from one mother's heart as an offering of ideas which I've used to teach my own children at home, and other people's children in schools, community centers and places of worship.

Since my teaching background draws from more than twenty years of working with the performing and creative arts, I have sought to approach the spiritual life using the arts as a pathway.

Chapters One: *Expressing Harmony* and Nine: *Developing Balance* both make use of creative movement as a tool for balancing body, mind and spirit. Chapter Eight: *Appreciating Beauty* uses the visual arts as a creative means of exploring the bounty of earth's blessings.

Stories and storytelling are essential teachers in most lessons, particularly Chapters Five: *Celebrating Community* and Six: *The Adventure of Human Awareness*. These lessons approach the study of history through an emphasis on empathy and personal experience. Music and song as vehicles for awareness, praise and thanksgiving are used in most chapters, and cultivating the musical life is addressed in Chapter Ten: *Creating Joy*.

The reader is encouraged to make use of this curriculum in the manner which most suits your children's sensibilities and your own interests. I suggest reading through the lessons and highlighting the activities that seem most workable for you. Activities are appropriate for all ages unless otherwise indicated. If any lesson stimulates your own variation or adaptation on the theme, I encourage you to venture out and go with your instincts. Be creative, use the lessons as a template. I would be delighted to hear about your own adaptations and suggestions.

Children learn what they see. All the best ideas in the universe are not as powerful as the small acts of love and kindness we can offer daily in our lives. Making a commitment to the spiritual growth of our children means we too learn to live with gratitude and compassion, moment to moment.

Expressing Harmony

Sound the note. Dance for joy.
Let the body be a prayer.
Through movement and sacred sound,
let children know great harmony.

Children love to move. They wiggle, jump, squirm, stretch, run, push, roll and reach. Their bodies are their primary instruments of expression and communication, and movement is a child's first language.

As educators, we can learn to trust this basic language of expression, which begins with the internal rhythm of breathing and expands into a world of boundless choices as the body moves through space.

Since dance has long been a vehicle for aligning body, breath and Spirit, we can draw from the traditions of creative dance combined with those of Sacred Music to help our children experience a deep sense of harmony within themselves.

Creative movement gives children the freedom to dance their own dances, within an atmosphere of acceptance and playful interaction. Sacred Music fills that creative environment with uplifting music of praise and devotion. This blend of music and movement provides a joyful way for children to sense and express the powerful resonance of heaven and earth through their own bodies.

The following lessons are designed to provide an opportunity to assist children in aligning body, mind and Spirit through movement and music. In each exploration, Sacred Music sets an inspirational and uplifting atmosphere for balancing children's physical bodies with universal harmonies. (For music selections, please see Resources at the end of this chapter.)

Harmony Dances

YOU WILL NEED: various selections of music from sacred traditions around the world (see Resources), a tape or CD player, a variety of colorful scarves or ribbons (12" pieces of wide, satin ribbon work best).

The person leading this movement activity should participate along with the group. Read through the process several times on your own first, until you can lead the activity without having to rely on reading it aloud.

WAKING UP THE BODY

Invite children to form a circle, standing up. Make sure each person has enough room to move.

Let's begin with a simple warm-up game of shaking out body parts: right arm, forward, backward, out to the side, up, down, all around.

Now shake out the other arm: forward, backward, etc.

Gently shake out one leg, forward, backward, etc., then the other leg.

Gently scratch all around one's hair to wake up the head.

Twist around to one side, letting the arms follow along and wrap around the body.

Twist to the other side. Repeat in a relaxed way both sides.

BREATHING STRETCH

Reach up to the sky as you breathe in (inhale).

Stretch way up toward the sky, reaching your arms all the way up above your head.

Now breathe out and let the upper body bend and fall forward, arms dangling down towards the floor, head relaxed, eyes facing knees.

Breathe in again and slowly reach back upwards toward the sky, stretching everything upwards, standing on tiptoes as you reach.

Exhale and let your body bend forward to meet the earth.

Now slowly roll up until you are standing straight up again.

GROWING ROOTS AND BRANCHES – Ages 5 and up

Make sure there's some space between your two feet as you are standing. Imagine yourself like a strong tree standing tall in a forest, with roots running through your legs and feet, deep into the

center of the earth. With your knees slightly bent, feel the power of the earth moving upward into your feet, legs, hips and trunk.

Imagine your body like a tree trunk, reaching upward with your arms growing out as branches through the sky.

Now feel a very gentle wind blowing around your arms, like a breeze around the branches. Let your whole body gently sway in whatever way the gentle breeze pushes your arms. Your hands and fingers can shake softly like leaves.

FALLING INTO STILLNESS

Now in very slow motion, like a leaf being carried by the wind, gently let your whole body fall down to the earth, very slowly until your whole body is resting on the ground. Allow your body to be completely still for a few moments, while the ground supports your body weight.

MOVEMENT AND MUSIC HARMONY: SCARF PLAY

With everyone settled, bring out a box with different colored scarves and/or ribbons and allow children to choose a scarf or ribbon.

After choosing their scarf, let each child find a place in the room where there is enough room to move freely.

Explain to the children that they can move any way they would like when they hear the music.

Put on a selection of music and encourage children to listen to the music with their whole bodies.

Imagine you could hear the music with any part of your body, not just your ears. Listen and dance with your hands, arms, feet, legs, back, etc.

Now let your scarves dance through the air as you listen and dance with your whole body.

GROUP VARIATIONS

If space is limited, or there is a very large group, you can divide the group into two smaller groups. One group dances, while the other group watches. Then switch roles.

TOSS AND CATCH

Scarves can be thrown in the air and "caught" with different body parts. Try tossing and catching with one body part at a time: elbows, knees, head, feet, etc.

This can be done independently, or with a partner (one scarf), trio (two scarves) or group (several scarves).

HARMONY ON CHAIRS

For groups that have less range of lower body support, are in wheel-chairs or if you just prefer to present a different option, arrange a circle of chairs with enough room between to stretch arms and fingers.

Without any props, first let the group listen to some selections of music, with eyes closed.

As you listen to the music, begin to let your arms and hands paint imaginary pictures in the air all around your upper body.

Experiment with dancing with just one finger… the whole right hand… left hand… both hands… hands and arms… just the head. Paint and carve through the space above the head, behind the back or wherever the range of motion is possible.

The following movement explorations help children gain experience as both leaders and followers, developing a strong feeling of cooperation and mutual respect.

MIRRORS OF HARMONY – Ages 6 and up

Arrange group into pairs, or have each person choose a partner. In the case of odd numbered groups, the facilitator participates as a partner. Partners face one another. Make sure there is enough space for everyone to move.

One person will begin as the *leader*. As the music is played, the leaders' job is to move freely in any way they choose, continuing to face their partner.

The other partner moves as the *mirror* image, trying to do the same movements as their partner, at the same time, as accurately as possible.

This ideally should look as if the leaders are looking in a full length mirror, with their mirror-self reflecting their movements.

Don't worry about how the movements look, just try to move in total harmony with your partner.

After three to five minutes, partners switch roles.

Facilitator signals the role changing again, several times, with shorter intervals in between.

If possible, ultimately, there is no leader or follower, just an ongoing flow of movement the partners create together in harmony with one another, and with the music.

GROUP CIRCLE HARMONY – Ages 6 and up

Mirroring can occur with the whole group working together.

Stand together in a circle with enough room between people so that everyone can move freely.

One person begins as the *leader*, moving freely to music, while the others face the leader and try to follow the leader's movements with their own bodies, moving in harmony as *mirrors*.

After a few minutes, pass the leadership to the next person in the circle, until each member has had a chance to lead, with others trying to follow as closely as possible.

It helps to vary this exercise by asking each *leader* to concentrate on dancing with certain body parts, such as head, shoulders, arms, hands, torso, legs or feet.

This exercise can be very playful while developing group attunement and trust.

ONE: Expressing Harmony

The following is a list of some ideas for music from sacred traditions. Any music that celebrates the human spirit can be used, so choose selections that might be part of the cultural background of your group.

Sacred Music selections from Western traditions:

Bach, Johann Sebastian. *Famous Choruses: The Sacred Cantatas.* Leonhardt - Consort, Gustav Leonhardt. Teldec Classics,1993.

Hazanout. *Chants liturgiques juifs. (Jewish Religious Vocal Music.)* Paris: Maison des Cultures du Monde, 1988.

Hildegard, Saint. *Sequences and Hymns by Abbess Hildegard of Bingen.* Gothic Voices with Emma Kirkby and Christopher Page. London: Hyperion, 1986.

Hildegard, Saint. *Vision: The Music of Hildegard von Bingen.* Angel, 1994. *A contemporary interpretation of the mystic melodies of Hildegard.*

Joel Cohen, cond., Boston Camerata. *The Sacred Bridge.* (France): Erato, 1990. *Jews and Christians in Medieval Europe.*

Vivaldi, Antonio and J. S. Bach. *Gloria in D Major and Magnificat in E flat major.* Choir of Christchurch Cathedral, Oxford. The Academy of Ancient Music. L'Oioseau - Lyre. London: Decca, 1979.

Expressing Harmony

Selections from World Music and eclectic traditions:

Africa Never Stands Still. Ellipsis Arts, 1994. *A collection of African music from 25 nations.*

Enya. *Shepherd Moons.* Reprise/Warner, 1991.

Global Harmony. *Music from the Heart.* The Relaxation Co., 1992.

Khan, Ali Akbar. *Garden of Dreams.* Worldly Music, 1993. *Classical Indian Ragas.*

Khechog, Nawang. *Sounds of Inner Peace.* Visions of Creative Peace, 1991. *Traditional Tibetan bamboo flute.*

Kitaro. *Light of the Spirit.* Geffen Records, 1987.

McKennitt, Loreena. *The Mask and Mirror.* Warner Brothers Records, 1994.

Nakai, R. Carlos. *Earth Spirit: Native American Flute Music.* Canyon, 1987.

Ni Riain, Noirin. *Soundings.* Cork, Ire.: Ossian Publications, 1993. *Spiritual Vocal Classics from many traditions including Celtic, Indian, Shaker songs and more.*

Nusrat Fateh Ali Khan on *Global Meditation: Harmony and Interplay.* The Relaxation Co., 1992.

Pomerantz, Lauren. *Wings of Time: The Sephardic Legacy of Multi-Cultural Spain.* Songbird Music, 1994.

Voices: *A Compilation of the World's Greatest Choirs.* Mesa/Bluemoon, 1990.

Vollenweider, Andreas. *Caverna Magica.* CBS Masterworks, Sony, 1983.

Expressing Harmony

For Sacred and World Music, check your local libraries, bookstores, music stores and the following mail-order catalogues:

Sacred Spirit Music, 5 Abode Road, New Lebanon, NY 12125, 800-794-6336

Alcazar, P.O. Box 429, Waterbury, VT 05676, 800-541-9904

Sounds True Audio, 735 Walnut Street, Boulder, CO 80302, 800-333-9185

Ladyslipper, P.O. Box 3124, Durham, NC 27715, 800-634-6044

Books for adults:

Benzwie, Teresa. *A Moving Experience: Dance for Lovers of Children and the Child Within.* Illus. Robert Bender. Tucson: Zephyr Press, 1987.

Bonheim, Jalaja. *The Serpent and the Wave: A Guide to Movement Meditation.* Berkeley: Celestial Arts, 1992.

Joyce, Mary. *First Steps in Teaching Creative Dance.* 3rd ed. Mountain View, CA: Mayfield Publishing, 1994.

Mettler, Barbara. *Materials of Dance as a Creative Art Activity.* Tucson: Mettler Studios, 1974.

Cultivating Mindfulness

Cultivate mindfulness.
See gratitude as a daily practice.
In pictures, words and songs, let children express a grateful heart.

Mindfulness is the process of paying attention, moment to moment, to one's thoughts, actions and surroundings without judgment or reaction, but with gratitude and joy. Mindfulness is a quality of attention which can be taught. Children as well as adults can be encouraged to notice the world around them, and to become aware of the thoughts and actions they are contributing to this world at any given moment.

Conscious awareness, or mindfulness, is an attribute of an awakened soul. How do we awaken the souls of our children? The first step is to realize that children are already in a heightened state of awareness. We need only to focus their sensitivity in a way which encourages appreciation and respect. We need to do less and allow more.

Gratitude is the way of mindfulness. When we begin to see and name the gifts we are given daily in our everyday lives, we plant the seeds of gratitude which will last a lifetime. In helping children develop a daily practice of giving thanks for each new morning, each still night, for the people who love and care for them, for the great abundance in their lives, we are enabling them to become mindful gardeners. They will then have the inner peace needed to cultivate seeds of love, compassion, joy, beauty and gratitude throughout their lives.

The following activities can help children express a grateful heart through creative art, words and songs.

GROWING A GRATEFUL HEART – Ages 4 and up; younger children will need assistance with writing ideas down.

YOU WILL NEED: pencils or pens and paper for brainstorming (chalkboard and chalk work well if available), large pieces of poster paper, oak tag or drawing paper, colored markers, coloring pencils and/or crayons.

DISCUSSION: Gather children in a comfortable setting. Ask them the question, *"What do you love having in your life?"* Brainstorming ideas can be written down by older children, or by adults for young children. Discuss all the gifts which surround each child in his/her world, including the people, family, friends, neighbors, home, favorite places, animals, things, foods, books, etc.

"ALL I LOVE" POSTER

Draw a huge heart on a large sheet of poster paper. Inside the heart write the words "I LOVE" or "I AM GRATEFUL FOR," and let the children write

in and/or illustrate all their favorite things. Young children can draw pictures. Let children include people, places, big and little things.

This works well as a collaborative group project, or each child can make a personal "Love" poster.

FAMILY OF LOVE COLLAGE – Ages 4 with assistance; older children can work independently.

YOU WILL NEED: photographs of each child, photos or parts of photos of their family members, favorite people, things, places, which can be cut and pasted; large piece of poster board for each child, glue stick, children's scissors.

Have children glue a photo of themselves in the middle of the paper. Allow children to choose other photographs, or parts of photos to glue around their photo to show what they love having around them.

When photo collages are complete, display them so children can appreciate all the blessings and bounty of their lives.

These photo collages also make great homemade gifts for special relatives or friends.

SEEDS OF GRATITUDE – Ages 4 with assistance and up

YOU WILL NEED: small potting trays, seed starter soil, packets of seeds – flowers, herbs or vegetables, watering cans, spoons or small trowels.

Ask each child to choose some seeds to plant. (Sunflower seeds work well because of their larger size.)

Prepare small pots or seed tray with seed-starter potting soil.

As each child plants a seed, ask them to bless that seed with love and plant a seed for something they are grateful for.

As the seeds are tended with water and grow, you can remind the children they are helping to keep the happy parts of their lives growing stronger.

For older children (nine or up), you can also suggest that they choose to plant a seed for a quality they would like to see grow stronger within themselves (patience, courage, acceptance, faith, joy, order, etc.).

Allow the indoor garden to be tended regularly, and weather permitting, you may transplant the seedlings outside if appropriate.

MORNING AND EVENING BLESSINGS – Ages 5 and up

YOU WILL NEED: two 5"x 7" blank index cards per child, markers or coloring instruments and pencils, hole puncher, piece of ribbon or string.

Create a morning and an evening blessing card for each child.

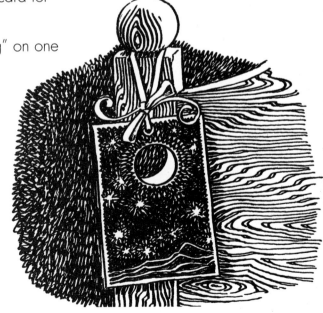

Have each child draw a picture of "morning" on one card, and "night" on the other card.

On the back of the morning picture, the child can write a special blessing for greeting the day.

For example, "Good Morning, World! I'm happy for another chance to… (child adds words like play, sing, work, jump, run, chat, hug, etc.)".

Children can draw a picture of themselves doing something they like doing in the morning.

For younger children, you can choose an inspirational poem or prayer for morning and write it on the card, leaving them space to illustrate or decorate as they like.

Do the same with evening card ("Good Night, World! Thank you for...").

Thread a ribbon through the top of each card, and hang it near the child's sleeping or special space, so child can adjust cards with the daily rhythms.

You will need to help younger children with blessing cards as appropriate.

SONGS OF GRATITUDE

Gather together in a circle to share songs that express a grateful heart. Choose a gesture or series of simple gestures to repeat during parts of the song, and have children join in with bodies and voices.

See Resources following this chapter for suggestions on where to find songs for children that celebrate life and express an appreciation of daily blessings.

TWO: Cultivating Mindfulness

Illustrated books for young children on morning blessings:

Baylor, Bird. *The Way to Start a Day*. New York: MacMillan, 1978.

Berger, Barbara. *When the Sun Rose*. New York: Philomel, 1990.

Charao, Kay. *The Baby's Good Morning Book*. New York: E.P. Dutton, 1986. *Poems, verses and rhymes by English and American poets.*

Marzollo, Jean. *Sun Song*. Illus. Laura Regan. New York: Harper Collins, 1995.

Swamp, Chief Jake. *Giving Thanks: A Native Good Morning Message*. Illus. Erwin Printup, Jr. New York: Lee & Low Books, 1995 (all ages).

Music and songs expressing gratitude and daily blessings:

    ✿ *indicates sound cassette or recording*
    △ *indicates printed songbook collection*

✿ "Beautiful Morning." Grammer, Red. *Can You Sound Just Like Me?* Smilin' Atcha Music, 1983.

△ Darian, Shea. *Seven Times the Sun: Guiding Your Child Through the Rhythms of the Day*. San Diego, CA: Lura Media, 1994. *A collection of songs, rituals and activities to celebrate daily life.*

△ "Day by Day" and 1200 songs of Faith, Love, Children and more in *Rise Up Singing: The Group Singing Songbook*. Blood, Peter and Annie Patterson, eds. Bethlehem, PA: A Sing Out! Publication,1988. ✿ Teaching tapes also available from publisher.

✿ "Each of Us is a Flower." Diamond, Charlotte. *10 Carrot Diamond*. Hug Bug Records, 1985.

✿ "Everything Grows." Raffi. *Everything Grows*. MCA Records, 1987.

✿ "Find a Peaceful Thought." Arnold, Linda. *Peace is the World Smiling*. Music for Little People, 1989.

✿ "First I Plant a Seed." Hull, Bunny. *A Child's Spirit*. Brassheart Music, 1994.

✿ "Love Grows One by One." Pease, Tom. *I'm Gonna Reach*. Tomorrow River Music, 1989.

△ "Morning has Broken" and many other songs of Thanksgiving, Love, Joy, Peace and more in *Praise for the Singing: Songs for Children*. Gill, Madelaine and Greg Pliska, colls. Boston: Little, Brown and Co., 1993.

✿ "Morning Song Chant." Brooke Medicine Eagle. *A Gift of Song*. Harmony Network, P.O. Box 9725, Berkeley, CA 94709.

✿ "Rise N' Shine." Raffi. *Rise N' Shine*. MCA Records, 1982.

△ ✿ "Say Thank You." Walters, J. Donald, comp. *All The World is My Friend: Songs, Stories, Activities and Piano Accompaniments*. Education for Life Foundation,1987. Also on the sound cassette *All the World is My Friend*. Education for Life Foundation. 14618 Tyler Foote Road, Nevada City, CA 95959.

✿ "Start the Day with Love." *Songs to the Goddess*. Sonoma County Birth Network, P.O. Box 1005, Occidental, CA 95465.

△ *Sing Through the Day: Ninety Songs for Younger Children*. Society of Brothers. Rifton, New York: Plough Publishing House, 1972.

✿ "Song to the Sun." Hall, Mary Gordon. *I Won't Go To Bed (Until I Sing My Song)*. Scooter Tunes, 1993. P.O. Box 6965, Charlottesville, VA 22906.

✿ "Thanks a Lot." Raffi. *Baby Beluga*. MCA Records, 1980.

△ "Thanks a Lot." reprinted in *2nd Raffi Songbook*. New York: Crown Publishers, 1987.

✿ "Things I'm Thankful For." Palmer, Hap. *Ideas, Thoughts, Feelings*. Educational Activities, n/d.

Illustrated books for young children on night blessings:

Berger, Barbara. *Grandfather Twilight*. New York: Philomel/Putnam Grosset, 1984.

Chorao, Kay. *The Baby's Bedtime Book*. New York: E.P. Dutton, 1984.

Fox, Mem. *Time for Bed*. Illus. Jane Dyer. New York: Harcourt Brace/Gulliver Books, 1993.

Hague, Michael, ed. *Sleep, Baby, Sleep: Lullabies and Night Poems*. New York: Morrow Junior Books, 1994.

Activities for older children:

Caduto, Michael & Joseph Bruchac. *Keepers of the Night: Native American Stories and Nocturnal Activities for Children*. Illus. David K. Fadden. Golden, CO: Fulcrum Publishing, 1994.

Music and songs for evening blessings:

✿ Ballingham, Patricia. *Earth Mother Lullabies From Around the World*, Vol. 1,2,3. EMP Records.

✿ Collins, Judy. *Baby's Bedtime*. (Companion to Kay Chorao's *The Baby's Bedtime Book*.) Lightyear Records, 1990.

✿ "Day is Done." Peter, Paul & Mary. *Best of Peter, Paul & Mary: 10 Years Together.* Warner Bros., 1970.

✿ Freyda. *Globalullabies*, Music for Little People, 1995.

✿ Herdman, Priscilla. *Star Dreamer: Nightsongs and Lullabies.* Alacazam, 1991.

✿ *Lullabye: A Collection.* Music For Little People, 1993. Includes Lorenna McKennit, Ladysmith Black Mambazo, Derek Bell and others.

✿ *Till Their Eyes Shine: The Lullabye Album.* Columbia, 1994.

✿ "Together Tomorrow." Chapin, Tom. *Family Tree.* Sony, 1988.

✿ "Sabunana Kusasa - We Will Meet Tomorrow." Pease, Tom. *Boogie! Boogie! Boogie!* Tomorrow River Music, 1985.

✿ "Wherever You Go, I Love You." Cassidy, Nancy. *Kid's Songs Sleepyheads.* Klutz Press, 1992.

✿ *World Sings Goodnight: Lullabies Sung in Native Voices.* Silver Wave Records, 1994.

Illustrated prayers and blessing collections for children:

Chorao, Kay, coll. *The Book of Giving: Poems of Thanks, Praise and Celebration.* New York: Dutton Children's Books, 1995.

Le Tord, Bijou, coll. *Peace on Earth: A Book of Prayers from Around the World.* New York: Bantam Doubleday Dell Publishing, 1992.

Stoddard, Sandol, comp. *Prayers, Praises, and Thanksgivings.* Illus. Rachel Isadora. New York: Dial Books, 1992.

Christian Tradition:

Bassin, Jenna, and Jane Lahr, eds. *A Garden of Prayer: A Family Treasury*. Illus. Juli Rauer. New York: Philosophical Library, 1989.

L'Engle, Madeleine. *Anytime Prayers*. Photos by Maria Rooney. Wheaton, IL: H. Shaw, 1994.

Walsh, Caroline, ed. *The Little Book of Prayers*. Illus. Inga Moore. New York: Kingfisher, 1993.

Yeatman, Linda, ed. *A Child's Book of Prayers*. Illus. Tracey Williamson, New York: Stewart, Tabori & Chang, 1992.

Jewish Tradition:

Edwards, Michelle. *Blessed are You: Traditional Everyday Hebrew Prayers*. New York: Lothrop, Lee & Shepard, 1993.

Groner, Judyth and Madeline Wikler. *Thank You, God! A Jewish Child's Book of Prayers*. Illus. Shelley O. Haas. Rockville, MD: Kar-Ben Copies, 1993.

Recommended reading on mindfulness for adults:

Bender, Sue. *Everyday Sacred*. San Francisco, CA: Harper San Francisco, 1995.

Epstein, Alan. *How to Be Happier Day by Day: A Year of Mindful Actions*. New York: Viking Penguin, 1993.

Kabat-Zinn, Jon. *Wherever You Go, There You Are: Mindfulness Meditation in Everyday Life*. New York: Hyperion, 1994.

Krishnamurti, J. *Freedom from the Known*. New York: Harper & Row, 1975.

Levine, Stephen. *A Gradual Awakening*. New York: Anchor Doubleday, 1979.

Cultivating Mindfulness

Nhat Hanh, Thich. *Touching Peace: Practicing the Art of Mindful Living*. Berkeley: Parallax Press, 1992.

Nhat Hanh, Thich. *The Miracle of Mindfulness*. Boston: Beacon Press, 1992.

Nhat Hanh, Thich. *Present Moment, Wonderful Moment: Mindfulness Verses for Daily Living*. Berkeley: Parallax Press, 1990.

Steindl-Rast, David. *Gratefulness, the Heart of Prayer: An Approach to Life in Fullness*. New York: Paulist Press, 1984.

Welwood, John, ed. *Ordinary Magic: Everyday Life as Spiritual Path*. Shambhala, 1992.

NOTES

Being of Service

Be not selfish, but selfless.
Give in the spirit of love,
Through caring actions and good works.

To be of service to others is the path of love in action. Yet, in general, our children are not always shown that to consider the good of the whole, to consider the needs of others, is an important step in being a responsible human being.

In this lesson, children are reminded of the need to help, without judgment or expectation of reward, simply because it is our human responsibility to take care of one another. By becoming active helpers in a world needing our attention, our children learn to feel the powerful presence of Love, not only through silent contemplation and prayer, but through action and work.

We learn most clearly about service through the process of being a caring family. In our moment to moment tasks, we show our children how families take care of one another. In a family, parents, grandparents, children and members of our chosen or extended families all have their own way of contributing to the good of the whole — caring for children, maintaining the home, working to support the family.

Ideally, it is within the home that children learn to care and be kind toward one another, not just on designated "Mother's" or "Father's" days, but

as a way of life. As parents and caregivers, we need to practice maintaining a conscious awareness of giving in the spirit of love, without expectation or reward.

"What can I do to help?" is a good question to practice asking one another. When we do our daily tasks at home with this awareness, it is a logical step to move our caring spirit beyond the home and into our communities, indeed our planet.

This can begin as simply as including children in the work we do. *"I'm folding this laundry so you and your brother can have fresh, clean clothes to wear. Would you like to help?"*

"Let's pick up the wrappers on our neighbor's yard while we are cleaning up here."

"We're going shopping for food; shall we ask Grandma (Mrs. Rose, etc.) if she needs something?"

If children at a young age see how we help one another, they will become aware of how their actions can help to meet the needs of the larger community of which they are a part. Then it is an inner awareness which tells them we are all responsible for taking care of one another. In addition, this practical approach to helping others draws on children's natural love of real work, and their sense of pride in accomplishing meaningful tasks in the world around them.

The following lessons are designed to enable children to learn how helping others benefits a greater good, and to expand their personal sphere of

family to include their community and the world around them.

You will need to gauge the level of participation for the children you are working with. I have included ideas that can be adapted to many ages. Even the youngest children appreciate helping to clean up their environment with others, or bringing something they've made to someone who appreciates their efforts.

HOW CAN I HELP?

DISCUSSION: Prepare the children for a visit to a place where people are in need (of company, physical assistance, etc.) by asking them, *"What does it mean to be of service?"* If children can read, write the word down; otherwise just sharing an informal discussion will work. The following are some examples:

What does it means when we say we need service?

–At a restaurant, gas station, etc.

What does a wait person say when they come to your table?

–May I help you?

To really be of service to another means to help that person. There are many ways we can help each other in our world. Can you think of a time when you needed help with something?

–Learning to walk, tying a shoe, carrying packages, doing homework.

Who helped you?

– Parents, friends, siblings.

Did you ever give someone help when they needed it?

– Picking up something that fell, helping with younger children.

Imagine if you couldn't do something for yourself; you might need some help to get something you wanted done. There are many people in our world who need extra help, and there are many people who work very hard helping others. Sometimes people get paid to help others, and sometimes people just help because they want to make the world a better place for everyone.

Whatever age you happen to be, there is something you can do to help others. It's also very important to remember that the best help you can give is help that supports a person to do something for her or himself. Sometimes just being with someone is all the help they need. Being of service also means taking care of our environment, at home, school, community and the planet we call home. After all, the earth is mother to us all.

Brainstorm with children about some ways they can be of help in their family, neighborhood, school classroom, etc.

RESCUE WAGONS: OPERATION HELPING MOTHER EARTH

YOU WILL NEED: a small wagon (old radio flyer wagons work well) or cart that can hold a cardboard box and plastic bags; a cardboard box, small enough for the wagon; plastic bags for collecting trash, old gloves or kid's garden gloves, art materials for decorating boxes.

Invite the children to go on a "Rescue Mission" for Mother Earth. You may want to read *Mother Earth* by Nancy Luenn or similar book (see Resources at the end of this chapter) as an introduction to the concept of earth as mother to all.

Decorate some wagons and cardboard boxes with messages and images about taking care of the earth. Organize a recycling box for glass or cans and another to hold plastic bags for collecting garbage.

Let children go on a clean-up mission with adult supervision to help pick up trash in an area surrounding your environment or a community area nearby. Wearing gloves is a good idea if children are going to pick up paper, etc. Warn young children not to pick up broken glass or sharp cans. After picking up in a designated area, help children decide what to do with their collection. Garbage gets thrown out, while cans, bottles, newspapers and some paper can be recycled.

If your community does not have a recycling program, call your local town hall to find out where you can bring items for recycling.

You can do this activity on a regular basis, and ask the children to name their rescue mission team; you can even design buttons or badges for children to sew onto a jacket or t-shirt.

Every day offers an opportunity to take care of Mother Earth. Encourage children to take care of her as a daily practice, not just on special rescue days.

HOW CAN I HELP? – Ages 7 and up

Decide on a place you could take the children either for a single visit or for a series of volunteer work days. Children can help serve food at a soup kitchen, share stories or songs with elders or help with simple tasks for an injured person.

There are many community-sponsored volunteer projects. Call your local library, church or temple. You can also contact an organization directly and ask to speak with the person in charge of volunteers.

(For more ideas, see Chapter 7: *Nourishing Compassion*.)

HELPING OUR ANIMAL FRIENDS – Ages 5 and up

DISCUSS with children some of the ways animals have helped people throughout history: oxen and horses for work, birds that deliver messages or hunt, dogs trained to help the blind or rescue people, dolphins who have

helped the emotionally and physically challenged, animals who offer companionship and comfort to people, etc.

What are some ways we can be of service to animals?

STORY: HELP FOR A HAWK

The following story tells how a six-year-old boy helped a very special red-tailed hawk.

Avalon was a six-year old boy who loved animals. He was visiting his favorite nature center one dcy, when he met a red-tailed hawk named Gypsy. Avalon learned that Gypsy would never be able to live in the wild again because of what had happened to her as a baby hawk.

When Gypsy was a very small bird, some young children took Gypsy from her nest in the wild and brought her to their home. The family kept the baby hawk inside as a pet, and fed her what they thought she would like to eat: hamburger meat. They didn't know that hawks need to eat the animals they hunt because nature provides exactly the right amount of nutrition in the bones and muscles of the animals they catch for hawks to grow strong. After a time, Gypsy got too big for the family to care for and they brought her to the Audubon Nature Center.

By this time, Gypsy had developed a disease called *rickets*, which affects bone growth, and she could no longer fly or walk properly. When

Avalon met Gypsy, she was living at the center as a "teaching" animal, and she was often taken to schools to teach children about hawks, and to help them learn how important it is to keep wild animals in their natural habitats.

Avalon was deeply moved by Gypsy's wild beauty and her story. Because it costs much money to take care of animals like Gypsy, the Nature Center offered people a way to "adopt" an animal by donating money to help feed and care for them. Avalon organized a one-boy campaign to raise enough money to adopt Gypsy for a year.

He cut out pictures of red-tailed hawks from nature magazines to make a poster that said, "SAVE A HAWK!" Then, with his mom, he went door to door talking to friends and neighbors about Gypsy's plight and asking for contributions to help adopt the hawk. He also added his own savings from money he made doing chores.

Soon Avalon had enough money to "adopt" Gypsy, and he gleefully brought his bag of coins and bills to the Nature Center so they could count on his support to help feed Gypsy for another year. The Audubon Nature Center had never had a young boy adopt an animal all on his own, and the Director of the Children's programs told the local newspaper about Avalon's campaign.

A newspaper reporter interviewed Avalon for a story in the local paper, and a photographer took a picture of him wearing leather protective gloves holding Gypsy.

It was exciting for Avalon to see his picture in the Sunday paper and read the story about Gypsy, but he says he didn't do it for that reason. He just wanted to help Gypsy and to let people know they can help hawks or any other animal by understanding what animals need to live.

DISCUSSION: *What happened to Gypsy when she was a baby?*
Should people take wild animals home as pets?
How can we help animals like Gypsy?

FINDING FURRY & FEATHERED FRIENDS

You may find a nature center that your child or group can visit. Many nature centers have programs to help teach children about what they can do to help animals. Older children can volunteer in the actual tending of animals while younger children learn by developing an appreciation for animal diversity and habitat.

Ask the people who care for the animals what you can do to help your animal friends.

HOW CAN I HELP MY ELDERS?

Discuss with children the need to honor and respect the people in their lives who have lived a long time and are wise from their life experiences. Have children share names of their grandparents or other elder relatives, and talk about the kinds of things they like to do together.

Older people sometimes need special care. *What are some things that people might need help with as they get older? How can you help?*

BEING OF SERVICE: SENIOR CELEBRATION – Ages 5 and up

YOU WILL NEED: any recycled party goods you may have, or children can make paper chain decorations using old magazines cut into strips; healthy snacks, apple treats, popcorn, mini-muffins, etc.; tape player and lively music (see Resources), joke books, puppets to dance to the music, etc.

Choose a date and place to have a party for special seniors. Children can invite grandparents, relatives, family friends or neighbors. Each child can ask their elder friend to share one special song, funny story, joke or poem. The group can also organize a sing-a-long of favorite songs to sing all together.

You can decide to create a party-in-a-box and bring it along with your group to a community senior center. Check with the person in charge of volunteers regarding how your group can help coordinate a celebration.

MAKE A TAPE OF JOY

YOU WILL NEED: blank tape/s (30 or 60 minutes), tape recorder, quiet space for recording.

Children of any age can bring joy to others by recording a tape of stories, songs, poems, riddles or jokes. A tape can be given to someone bedridden, unable to read or anyone in need of cheer.

As a group, choose a person for whom you would like to make a tape. Practice singing some songs you can record on the tape. Decide on what else you would like to record, and in what order. Older kids can read stories on the tape, and younger children can tell about a favorite adventure. It's really up to the imaginations of your children to create an enjoyable listening hour for someone.

MEETING PEOPLE WHO SERVE OTHERS

Collect stories of historical figures who have done something to help others. Be on the watch for news stories of young people who have made a difference by their actions. Read these together with the children.

Create a collage or bulletin board with photos and stories of real people who care. (For further ideas on being of service, see Chapter Seven: *Nourishing Compassion*.)

THREE: Being of Service

See also Resources for Chapter Seven: Nourishing Compassion.

Illustrated books for young children on caring and helping:

Ancona, George. *Helping Out.* Boston, MA: Houghton Mifflin, 1991.

Fox, Mem. *Wilford Gordon McDonald Partridge.* Illus. Julie Vivas. Brooklyn, NY: Kane/Miller, 1985.

Fyleman, Rose. *A Fairy Went A-Marketing.* New York: Dutton, 1986.

Graham, Bob. *Rose Meets Mr. Wintergarten.* Cambridge, MA: Candlewick Press, 1992.

Hughes, Shirley. *Giving.* Cambridge, MA: Candlewick Press, 1995.

Luenn, Nancy. *Mother Earth.* Illus. Neil Waldman. New York: Aladdin/Simon & Schuster, 1995.

Osofsky, Audrey. *My Buddy.* Illus. Ted Rand. New York: Henry Holt & Co., 1992. *How a companion guide dog helps a young physically challenged boy.*

Schimmel, Schim. *Dear Children of the Earth: A Letter from Home.* Minocqua, WI: North Word Press, 1994.

Silverstein, Shel. *The Giving Tree.* New York: Harper Collins, 1964.

Books for children:
Ages 8 and up

Goodman, Alan. *The Big Help Book: 365 Ways You Can Make a Difference by Volunteering.* Illus. Fiona Smyth. New York: Pocket Books, 1994.

Goodman, Billy. *A Kid's Guide to How to Save the Animals.* New York: Avon Books, 1991.

Goodman, Billy. *A Kid's Guide to How to Save the Planet.* Illus. Paul Meisel. New York: Avon Books, 1990.

Conari Press Ed. *Kids Random Acts of Kindness.* Berkely, CA: Conari Press, 1994.

Kibbey, Marsha. *The Helping Place.* Illus. Jennifer Hagerman. Minneapolis, MN: Carolrhoda Books, Inc.,1991. *A look at the way a nursing home can serve elders.*

Koebner, Linda. *For Kids Who Love Animals: A Guide To Sharing the Planet.* Venice, CA: Living Planet Press, 1991.

Logan, Suzanne. *The Kids Can Help Book.* New York: Perigree Books - Putnam/Cloverdale Press, 1992.

Mayo, Gretchen Will. "Daylight Comes at Last" in *North American Indian Stories.* New York: Walker & Co, 1990. *Raven, the trickster, cleverly restores order for the good of the whole.*

Schwartz, Linda. *How Can You Help? Creative Volunteer Projects for Kids Who Care.* Illus. Beverly Armstrong. Santa Barbara, CA: Learning Works, 1994.

Humor:

Cole, Joanna and Stephanie Calmenson, comps. *The Laugh Book: A New Treasury of Humor for Children.* Illus. Marylin Hafner. New York: Doubleday, 1986.

Young, Frederica. *Super-Duper Jokes.* Illus. Chris Murphy. New York: Farrar Straus & Giroux, 1993.

Being of Service

Music and songs for children on being of service:

✿ *indicates sound cassette or recording*
△ *indicates printed songbook collection*

✿ "All the World is My Friend." Walters, Donald. *All the World is My Friend.* Education for Life Foundation, 1987.

✿ "Helping." Thomas, Marlo & Friends. *Free to Be...You and Me.* Arista, 1972.

✿ "Thank Someone." Thomas, Marlo & Friends. *Free To Be a Family.* A & M, 1988.

✿ "The Giving Tree." Cowboy Steff. *The Giving Tree & Other Shel Silverstein Songs.* Sony, 1992.

✿ "There's Always Something You Can Do." Pirtle, Sarah. *Two Hands Hold The Earth.* A Gentle Wind, 1984.

✿ "To Be a Friend." Crow, Dan. *A Friend, a Laugh, a Walk in the Woods.* Sony, 1992.

Books for adults:

Caduto, Michael and Joseph Bruchac. *Keepers of the Animals: Native American Stories and Wildlife Activties for Children.* Illus. John K. Fadden (Ka-Ho-Nes). Golden, CO: Fulcrum Publishing, 1991.

Caduto, Michael and Joseph Bruchac. *Keepers of the Earth.* Illus. John Kahiones Fadden. Golden, CO: Fulcrum Publishing, 1988.

Hopkins, Susan. *Discovering the World: Empowering Children to Value Themselves, Others and the Earth.* Philadelphia: New Society Publishers, 1990.

Johnson, Cait and Maura D. Shaw. *Celebrating the Great Mother: A Handbook of Earth-Honoring Activities for Parents and Children.* VT: Destiny Books/Inner Traditions, 1995.

Reynolds, Rebecca A. *Bring Me the Ocean: Nature as Teacher, Messenger and Intermediary.* Acton, MA: VanderWyk & Burnham Publishing Co., 1995.

4

Fostering Self-Reliance

Honor the sacred circle of life.
Show children the connections between
themselves and the world they are a part of.
Foster responsibility about choices and actions.

What does it mean to be self-reliant?

As parents and teachers, we want our children to be able to take care of themselves, their personal belongings, their environments and shared communities. Although self-reliance implies a responsible independence, it is also about being able to maintain one's relation with the world.

If we can help children see how their actions and choices affect people, places, animals — indeed the well-being and future of their home planet, then as they become active participants in a larger community they will make decisions that will reflect a caring attitude toward themselves and others.

One can nourish self-reliance in children by reinforcing an appreciation of the connections between ourselves and the world around us. Many sacred traditions have made use of the circle as a symbol for this understanding of inclusiveness.

The sacred circle, the great wheel of life, the mandala and the Medicine Wheel of Native American wisdom are all paradigms of wholeness that reflect the understanding that independence is not based on an illusion

of separateness, but on the understanding of unity, cooperation and harmony.

Children are naturally inclusive, until through the acquisition of language, they begin to separate, name and judge. As educators, we understand the recognition of differences as a natural part of development, yet as parents and teachers, we can enable children to grow while helping them maintain an understanding of wholeness.

We need to see self-reliance as responsible cooperation, not me separate from you, separate from nature, Spirit, the people across the street or on the other side of the world, but as part of the whole continuum of life.

In this way, even watering the plants becomes an important task in contributing to the good of the whole. Fostering this awareness helps children see themselves as significant individuals, part of a collective greater than themselves. A child then begins to know Self in a harmonious relationship with family, community, humanity, nature, Spirit.

The following activities use nature to teach children an understanding of the interrelatedness of all life.

SEEING CONNECTIONS

Take the children on a walk and point out how everything in the natural world is interdependent: sun, plants, animals, etc. Pointing out or discussing the food chain can be useful here.

If you do not have access to a nature walk or path, bring in pictures which show this connection.

DISCUSSION: Ask child to look at a tree (or picture a tree).

What does the tree need to grow?

—Sun, rain, nourishment from the soil, etc.

What happens to the leaves when they wither and fall from the tree?

—They break down (decompose) and go back to the earth, to make the soil rich and strong so more trees can grow.

Nothing in nature is wasted.

Even animals that die are carrion (food) for other animals, and are used in the big circle of nature. This big circle of life is called a life-cycle, because like a circle, it goes round and round.

LIFE CYCLES – Ages 6 and up

YOU WILL NEED: poster board, or large drawing paper (18" x 24"), drawing tools, compass or large plates for tracing circles, pencil.

Draw a big circle on a posterboard or piece of paper. Encourage children to observe how in a circle there is no beginning or end; a circle goes around and around.

DISCUSSION:

Can you think of some LIFE CYCLES?

What about what we do every day?

— Waking, eating, working, playing, sleeping, waking…

SUMMER · FALL · WINTER · SPRING

MORNING · AFTERNOON · EVENING · NIGHT

PLANTING · GROWING · HARVESTING

BIRTH · LIFE · DEATH

– Morning, afternoon, evening…

– Fall, winter, spring, summer…

– Inhaling, exhaling…

– Planting, growing, harvesting…

– Birth, death, birth…

(You can use leaves falling from trees as an example.)

LIFE CYCLES POSTER – Ages 6 and up

Draw a series of concentric circles. Write the name of a life-cycle on each circle. Let children decorate each circle by choosing illustrations which show something about that particular process.

Life Cycle posters can be hung in classrooms or home and are a lovely reminder of the continuity of life.

WEB OF LIFE

DISCUSSION: *Animals, plants, people, all things are connected in the great circle of life. This connection can be imagined as a big web, linking all things together, so that what affects one system will eventually reach all the others.*

What are the things we all need to live?

– Sun, water, air, food…

What would happen without any of these things?

– No life.

Now think about a baby. Could a baby live without these things? A baby needs something more… someone to take care of her or him, to protect that baby so it can grow. What else do we need to grow? There is something everyone needs in order to live and grow, and that is love. Without love, people cannot be happy and grow strong. We all need love to feel connected, as a family, and in the bigger circles of our community and our world.

LIFE WEB – Ages 6 and up

YOU WILL NEED: a long piece of vine to twist into a hoop like a wreath (you can also use an embroidery hoop from a craft store), kite twine or thin string, needle and thread, a basket for each child to collect nature treasures for the web.

Connect the vine so it forms a large circle.

Attach string to vine or hoop in four places. Continue attaching the string around the hoop until you have created a web design.

Allow children to walk in a park, nature trail, backyard or similar environment, and with adult supervision, allow them to collect nature treasures in their baskets to attach to the Life Web: seed pods, small insect wings, pieces of fallen bark (don't pull bark off living trees), flower petals, leaves, seeds, etc. Remind children to only collect things that have already fallen.

If you are not in an area which allows for this kind of exploration, or weather doesn't permit outdoor activities, you might use old nature magazines to cut out pictures of wildlife, or children can draw small pictures to attach to the web.

Depending on the size of the group, you can make one web for the whole group to decorate, or one for each child. An adult will need to sew the found treasures onto the web's strings with needle and thread. Life Webs look wonderful in a window!

FOUR: Fostering Self-Reliance

Illustrated books for children on life cycles:

Burton, Virginia Lee. *Life Story.* Boston: Houghton Mifflin, 1962.

Cherry, Lynne. *The Great Kapok Tree: A Tale of the Amazon Rain Forest.* New York: Harcourt Brace Jovanovich, 1990.

Cooney, Barbara. *Island Boy.* New York: Viking Kestrel, 1988.

Curtis, Chara M. *All I See is Part of Me.* Illus. Cynthia Aldrich. Rev. ed. Bellevue, WA: Illumination Arts, 1994.

Gershator, David. *Bread is For Eating.* Illus. Emma Shaw-Smith. New York: Henry Holt & Co., Inc., 1995. *Text in English, Song Lyrics in English and Spanish. A tale of the cycles of life, family and community.*

Gerstein, Mordicai. *The Mountains of Tibet.* New York: Harper & Row, 1989. *A story of a human being looking at the cycle of life and death, and making choices.*

Griffin, Sandra Ure. *Earth Circles.* New York: Walker & Co. 1989.

Henderson, Kathy. *In the Middle of the Night.* Illus. Jennifer Eachus. New York: Trumpet Club, 1992.

Kalman, Bobbie and Janine Schaub. *I am a Part of Nature.* The Primary Ecology Series. New York: Crabtree Publishing Co., 1992.

Kandoian, Ellen. *Molly's Seasons*. New York: Cobblehill Books, 1992.

Lasky, Kathryn. *Pond Year*. Illus. Mike Bostock. Cambridge, MA: Candlewick Press, 1995.

Lesser, Carol. *The Goodnight Circle*. Illus. Lorinda Bryan Cauley. New York: Harcourt Brace Jovanovich, 1984.

Mazer, Anne. *The Salamander Room*. Illus. Steve Johnson. New York: Alfred A. Knopf, 1991.

Muller, Gerda. *Circle of Seasons*. New York: Dutton Children's Books, 1994.

Romanova, Natalia. *Once There was a Tree*. Illus. Gennadii Spirin. New York: Dial Books for Young Readers, 1989.

Schuett, Stacey. *Somewhere in the World Right Now*. New York: Knopf, 1995.

Seattle, Chief. *Brother Eagle, Sister Sky*. Illus. Susan Jeffers. New York: Dial Books, 1991.

Van Laan, Nancy. *In A Circle Long Ago. 25 Songs and Stories from Native American Tribes of North America*. Illus. Lisa Desmini. New York: Knopf/Apple Soup, 1995.

White Deer of Autumn. *The Great Change*. Illus. Carol Grigg. Hillsboro, OR: Beyond Words Publishing, 1994. *A look at death as transformation.*

Yolen, Jane. *Letting Swift River Go*. Boston: Little, Brown & Co., 1992.

Yolen, Jane. *Ring of Earth: A Child's Book of Seasons*. Illus. John Wallner. New York: Harcourt Brace Jovanovich, 1986. *Poetry and watercolors exploring the seasons.*

Zolotow, Charlotte. *When the Wind Stops*. Illus. Stefano Vitale. New York: Harper & Row, 1975.

Fostering Self-Reliance

Music and songs that honor the cycles of life:

✿ *indicates sound cassette or recording*
△ *indicates printed songbook collection*

✿ "All God's Critters Got a Place in the Choir." McCutcheon, John. *Howjadoo.* Rounder Records, 1987.

✿ "Circle of Life" John, Elton & Tim Rice. *The Lion King.* Walt Disney Music Co. ASCAP/Wonderland Music, 1994.

✿ "Down on the Farm." Scott, Molly. *Honor the Earth.* Fretless Records, 1980.

✿ "Everything Grows." Raffi. *Everything Grows.* MCA Records, 1987.

✿ "Green Grass Grows All Around." Seeger, Pete. *Abiyoyo and Other Story Songs for Children.* Smithsonian/Folkways, 1989.

✿ "Magical Earth." Pirtle, Sarah. *Magical Earth.* A Gentle Wind, 1993.

△ Mallet, David. *Inch by Inch: The Garden Song.* New York: Harper Collins, 1995.

✿ "Mother Earth's Routine." Chapin, Tom. *Mother Earth.* Sony, 1990.

✿ "One Light One Sun." Raffi. *One Light One Sun.* Shoreline/MCA Records, 1985 and in *The 2nd Raffi Songbook.* New York: Crown Publishers, 1987.

✿ "Rain Round." Rogers, Sally. *Piggyback Planet.* Round River Records, 1990.

✿ "Two Hands Hold the Earth." Pirtle, Sarah. *Two Hands Hold the Earth.* A Gentle Wind, 1984.

△ "We Circle Around," "The Green Grass Grows All Around," and "All God's Critters Got a Place in the Choir" in *Rise Up Singing: The Group-Singing Song Book.* Blood, Peter and Anne Blood-Patterson, ed. Bethlehem, PA: Sing Out! Publications, 1988.

✿ "Water Cycle Boogie." Banana Slug String Band. *Slugs at Sea.* Music for Little People, 1991.

Books for adults:

Cornell, Joseph. *Sharing Nature With Children*. Nevada City, CA: Dawn Publications, 1979. The Classic Parents' and Teachers' Nature Awareness Guidebook.

Cornell, Joseph and Michael Deranja. *Journey to the Heart of Nature: A Guided Exploration*. Nevada City, CA: Dawn Publications, 1994.

Lachecki, Marina and Carolyn Olson. *Teaching Kids to Love the Earth*. Duluth, MN: Pfeifer-Hamilton, 1991.

Lachecki, Marina and James Kasperson. *More Teaching Kids to Love the Earth*. Illus. Karyln Holman. Duluth, MN: Pfeifer-Hamilton, 1995.

Petrash, Carol. *Earthways: Simple Environmental Activities for Young Children*. Mount Rainier, MD: Gryphon House, 1992.

Sheehan, Kathryn and Mary Waidner. *Earthchild: Games, Stories, Activities, Experiments & Ideas about Living Lightly on Planet Earth*. Rev. ed. Tulsa, OK: Council Oak Books, 1994.

Storm, Hyemeyohsts. *Seven Arrows*. New York: Ballantine Books, 1985.

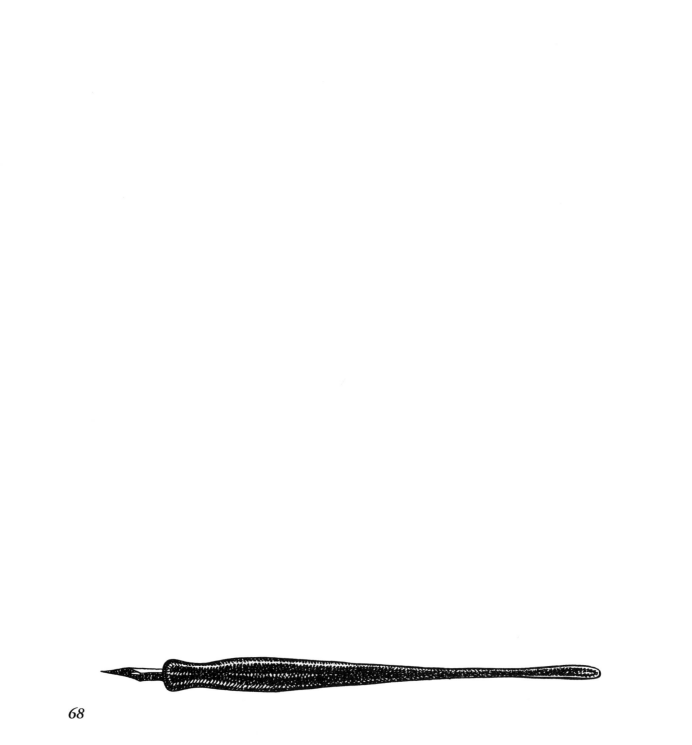

Celebrating Community

Plan your celebrations as a seasonal calendar,
not with small tasks and busywork,
but with a deep reverence for change.

*I*n celebrating together, a circle of unity is formed in which children see themselves in relation to the whole. Celebrations which move with the rhythms of Nature provide a deeper understanding of cycles, rhythms and the order of the universe.

A curriculum which is arbitrary, or based solely on developmental concepts, often lacks a connection with the planet upon which our lives depend. A curriculum which is coordinated with seasonal cycles has an integrity, a rootedness, a strength and logic based on that which all life depends—the earth.

Celebrations can grow from a simple rhythm of meals and family gatherings, to a grander, wider circle of festivals that involve a larger community.

Stories, songs, games, laughter—this is the thread of community. A people's celebrations are what gives them a sense of self, in relation to the movement of the earth, in relation to one another and to God.

These ideas for celebrations involve developing a respect for the changes of seasons and cycles in the context of community life.

PLAN A YEAR OF SEASONAL CELEBRATIONS

DISCUSSION:

What happens at different times of the year? How do we know it is winter? — Leaves fall off trees, snow falls, animals hide, etc.

What about spring… summer… fall…? Each season is a time for something different to happen on the earth. Just as our days have cycles, the year has a rhythm of its own, and living on the earth, we celebrate those different times in many different ways.

WHEEL OF CHANGE

YOU WILL NEED: large art paper, pencil, coloring tools.

Make a Wheel of Change using the illustration as a model, or create one of your own design. Place the holidays you choose to celebrate in your family or class. Include birthdays on the wheel, and any special occasions your group wants to honor.

Any day can be cause for celebration: First Snowfall Day, Rainy Boots Day, Quarter Moon Night, Butterfly Morning Breakfast, Everyday Earth Day, Popcorn and Pajamas Peace Picnic, Summer Lawn Tea, Pumpkin Harvest Fiesta.

There are no limitations to what you can celebrate. Create your own traditions, ceremonies, blessings and songs. Gather together to give thanks in harmony with the seasons and bounty of the earth. Prepare or share a meal, light a candle and say a prayer or poem, share stories and songs.

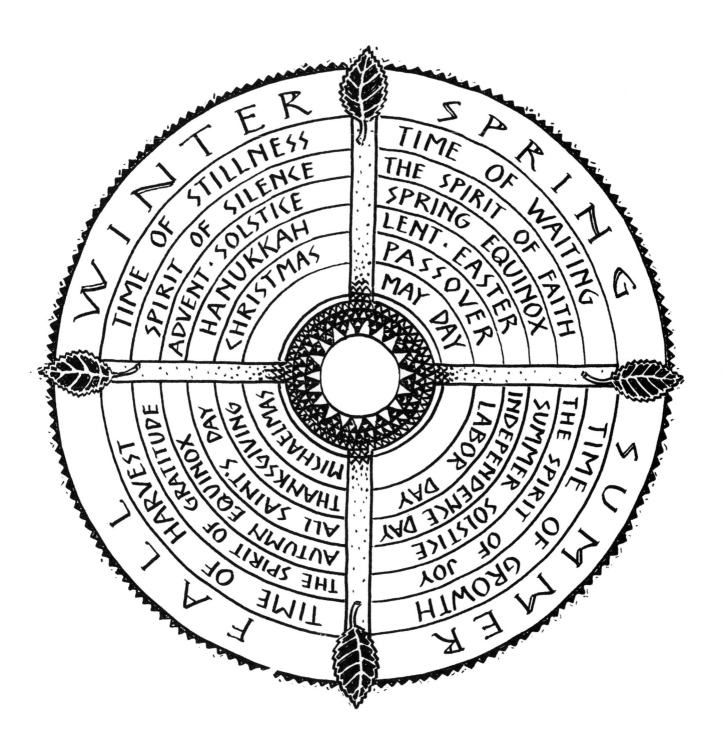

WINTER · SPRING · SUMMER · FALL

TIME OF STILLNESS
SPIRIT OF SILENCE
ADVENT · SOLSTICE
HANUKKAH
CHRISTMAS

TIME OF WAITING
THE SPIRIT OF FAITH
SPRING EQUINOX
LENT · EASTER
PASSOVER
MAY DAY

THE SPIRIT OF GRATITUDE
AUTUMN EQUINOX
ALL SAINT'S DAY
THANKSGIVING
MICHAELMAS

TIME OF HARVEST

SUMMER SOLSTICE
INDEPENDENCE DAY
LABOR DAY
THE SPIRIT OF JOY
TIME OF GROWTH

You can create an atmosphere of celebration with recorded or live music, and an open space to dance with joy.

The following list provides a starting point for developing a seasonal calendar of celebrations. Add your own important festivals and traditions which occur throughout the year.

WINTER: Time of Stillness
The spirit of Silence
In the midst of winter, the Light is revealed
Celebrations: Advent, St. Nicholas Eve, Christmas, Feast of the Epiphany, Midwinter Solstice, Candlemas, Hanukkah, Kwaanza

SPRING: Time of Waiting
The spirit of Faith
The promise of rebirth
Celebrations: Lent, Spring Equinox, Easter, May Day, Whitsun, Passover

SUMMER: Time of Growth
The spirit of Joy
The sense of fullness
Celebrations: Summer Solstice, Midsummer Festival

Celebrating Community

FALL: Time of Harvest
The spirit of Gratitude
The call of change
Celebrations: Autumn Equinox, Michaelmas, All Hallow's Eve, All Saint's •
Day, All Soul's Day, Thanksgiving, Succot

SIMPLE CELEBRATIONS – THE FAMILY MEAL

Sharing a meal may well be the most basic form of creating community. It is a coming together of family, friends, and a chance to give thanks for the bounty of the earth, the blessings of God, the joy of union.

Even the simplest of meals can have the spirit of celebration. Perhaps the most significant element is the sacred moment before the meal begins, the time known traditionally for "saying grace."

As adults, many of us have discarded, for various reasons, the seemingly formal act of saying grace before a meal. Now as parents or caregivers, we long for a means of having a sense of appreciation and peace take hold, for a moment, before food is consumed.

Sharing a blessing can be as simple as having everyone gathered hold hands for a moment to share a moment of silence, a prayer, poem or song. In our home, grace is often an adapted refrain from a traditional folk tune:

Oats and beans and barley grow
Oats and beans and barley grow
Do you or I or anyone know
* *How oats and beans and barley grow?*
Followed by a chorus of "Blessings on your meal!"

Going around the table having each person share something they are grateful for is also a lovely way to start a meal.

For more ideas on blessings see Resources at the end of this chapter.

CREATE A CENTER-PEACE

Creating the focal point or centerpiece of
the table can include seasonal displays,
requiring actions as simple as putting a newly
picked dandelion in a jelly jar of water.

There is something very special, however, in the act
of bringing light to the table in the form of candles. Lit
candles suggest the blessing of Spirit, the light of wisdom,
the flame of faith. As always, careful adult supervision is
required with candles.

Don't wait for special holidays to set the table in a
sacred manner. Any meal can be lifted to a feeling of

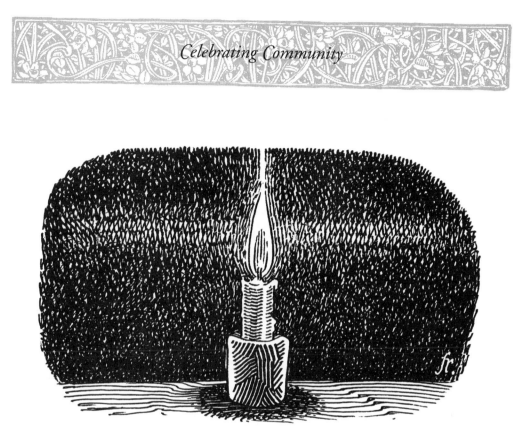

loving care with a vase of flowers, perhaps "the good" dishes, a tablecloth, whatever feels right in creating a harmonious sense of grace.

FAMILY/COMMUNITY MEETING

Start a tradition of a weekly or monthly family or community meeting. Determine a time and place to gather together and decide how you want to structure the event.

You can choose to begin and end the meeting with a consistent form, holding hands, lighting a candle, saying a prayer or sharing a song. Within the meeting make time for both business and the pleasure of just sharing fun.

Each member of the family can have an opportunity to share something, or raise an issue for discussion. Each member is given the space to speak without judgment or reaction.

Solutions can be worked out together, or guardians may need to make decisions and get back on certain considerations.

Meetings are a wonderful time to tell stories, work together on projects, listen to music, start a family newsletter or a journal. The possibilities are as wide as the imagination of your family or group.

See Resources for more ideas.

TELL STORIES ALL YEAR

Storytelling blends the magic of imagination with the warmth of shared experience. Any time of year is appropriate to share stories from your own life about holiday celebrations, seasonal memories or just favorite stories.

Children love to hear true stories. Anything can lead to a tale.

Here are some questions to get started with:

What does the smell of new shoes remind you of?

Can you recall a big snowstorm or thunderstorm when you were a child?

Where was your favorite summer swimming place or secret place?

What mischief did you get into with a friend?

What do you remember most about your grandmother's or elder's family gatherings?

FIVE: Celebrating Community

Illustrated picture books for children on celebrating life changes:

Baylor, Byrd. *I'm In Charge of Celebrations*. Illus. Peter Parnall. New York: Charles Scribner's Sons, 1986.

Frasier, Debra. *On the Day You Were Born*. Illus. Nancy Patz. New York: Harcourt Brace Jovanovich, 1991.

Jackson, Ellen. *Winter Solstice*. Illus. Jan D. Ellis. Brookfield, CT: Millbrook Press, 1994.

Varley, Susan. *Badger's Parting Gifts*. New York: Lothrop, Lee & Shepard, 1984.

Zagwyn, Deborah Turney. *The Pumpkin Blanket*. Berkeley: Celestial Arts, 1990.

Music and songs for seasonal celebrations:

    ✿ *indicates sound cassette or recording*
    △ *indicates printed songbook collection*

✿ "All of the Seasons." Whitely, Ken. *All of the Seasons*. Alacazam!, 1992.

✿ "Circle of the Sun." Rogers, Sally. *In the Circle of the Sun*. Thrushwood, n/d.

✿ "Four Seasons." Baron, Laura & Patti Dallas. *Songs for the Earth*. Golden Glow Records, 1992.

❁ "Harvest Blessing." Tickle Tune Typhoon. *Heart and Hands*. Tickle Tune Typhoon, 1991.

❁ "I Can't Wait for Spring." Pirtle, Sarah. *Wind Is Telling Secrets*. A Gentle Wind, 1988.

❁ "I Circle Around." Arapaho chant, in *Rise Up Singing Songbook* and on *Circle Around*. Tickle Tune Typhoon, 1983.

❁ "Seasons." Avni, Fran. *Daisies and Ducklings*. Lemonstone Records, 1990.

△ Society of Brothers. *Sing Through the Seasons: Ninety-Nine Songs for Children*. Illus. Susanna Biene. Rifton, NY: Plough Publishing House, 1972.

△ "Turn, Turn, Turn." Seeger, Pete, adapted. New York: Melody Trails, 1962.

Poetry collections:

Beskow, Elsa. *Around the Year*. Verses to Celebrate the Seasons. Gryphon House, 1988.

Foster, John, ed. *Let's Celebrate*. Festival Poems of All Cultures. Oxford University Press, 1990.

Books for children about celebrations:

Birch, Beverly. *Festivals*. Morristown, NJ: Silver Burdett Press, 1986. *International celebrations*.

Campbell, Louise. *A World of Holidays!* Illus. Michael Bryant. Family Ties Series. New York: Silver Moon Press, 1993.

Drucker, Malka. *The Family Treasury of Jewish Holidays*. Boston: Little, Brown & Co., 1994.

Greenberg, Melanie Hope. *Celebrations: Our Jewish Holidays*. Philadelphia: Jewish Publication Society, 1991.

Kalman, Bobbie. *The Holidays and Festivals Series*. Series includes *We Celebrate Winter, We*

Celebrate Spring, We Celebrate the Harvest, We Celebrate Family Days. New York: Crabtree Publishing, 1985–1986.

Smith, Debbie. *Holidays and Festivals Activities.* New York: Crabtree Publishing, 1994.

Illustrated books for children on family and community:

Aliki. *Communication.* New York: Greenwillow Books, 1993.

Cooper, Melrose. *I Got a Family.* Illus. Dale Gottlieb. New York: Henry Holt & Co., 1993.

Cooper, Melrose. *I Got Community.* New York: Henry Holt & Co., 1995.

Curtis, Chara M. *How Far to Heaven?* Bellevue, WA: Illumination Arts, Inc., 1993.

Friedman, Ina. *How My Parents Learned to Eat.* Illus. Allen Say. Boston: Houghton Mifflin Co., 1984. *A Japanese-American girl tells the story of how her parents met.*

Gershator, David. *Bread is for Eating.* New York: Henry Holt & Co., 1995. *In Spanish and English.*

Joosse, Barbara M. *Mama Do You Love Me?* San Francisco: Chronicle Books, 1991.

Kaiser Johnson, Lee and Sue Kaiser Johnson. *If I Ran the Family.* Illus. Roberta Collier-Morales. Minneapolis: Free Spirit, 1992.

MacLachlan, Patricia. *All the Places to Love.* Illus. Mike Wimmer. A Charlotte Zolotow Book. New York: Harper Collins, 1994.

McBratney, Sam. *Guess How Much I Love You.* Cambridge, MA: Candlewick Press, 1995.

Munsch, Robert. *Love You Forever.* Willowdale, Ont.: Firefly Books, 1986.

Shelby, Anne. *Homeplace.* Illus. Wendy A. Halperin. New York: Orchard Books, 1995.

Skutch, Robert. *Who's in a Family?* Illus. Laura Nienhaus. Berkeley: Tricycle Press, 1995.

Thomas, Marlo and Friends. *Free to Be... a Family.* New York: Bantam Books, 1987.

Williams, Mary L. *Let's Celebrate Our Differences.* Deerfield Beach, FL: Health Communications, Inc., 1994.

Yolen, Jane. *All Those Secrets of the World.* Boston: Little, Brown & Co, 1991.

Music and songs on family themes:

❀ "All I Really Need." Raffi. *Baby Beluga.* MCA Records, 1977.

❀ "Be Kind to Your Parents." Arnold, Linda. *Make Believe.* A & M Records, 1986.

❀ "Brothers and Sisters," Grammer, Red. *Do-Re-Mi.* Smilin' Atcha Music, 1991.

❀ "Families are Made of Love." Atkinson, Lisa. *One and Only Me.* A Gentle Wind, 1989.

❀ *Family Garden.* McCutcheon, John. Rounder Records, 1993.

❀ "Family Song." Tickle Tune Typhoon. *Hug the Earth.* Tickle Tune Typhoon, 1985.

❀ "Listen." Grammer, Red. *Teaching Peace.* Smilin' Atcha Music, 1986.

❀ "Love Grows One by One." Pease, Tom. *I'm Gonna Reach.* Tomorrow River Music, 1989.

❀ Thomas, Marlo and Friends. *Free To Be... A Family.* A & M Records, 1988.

Celebrating Community

Books for adults on creating celebrations and community:

Bland, Helen Baine and Mary S. Sears. *Celebrating Family Traditions: An Idea & Keepsake Book.* Boston: Little, Brown & Co., 1993.

Carey, Diana and Judy Large. *Festivals, Family and Food.* Stroud: Hawthorn Press, 1982. *A seasonal cornucopia of stories, songs, activities and recipes for celebrating holidays all through the year.* (Waldorf-based.)

Cunningham, Nancy B. *Feeding The Spirit: How to Create Your Own Ceremonial Rites, Festivals and Celebrations.* San Jose, CA: Resource Publications, 1988.

Darian, Shea. *Seven Times the Sun: Guiding Your Child Through the Rhythms of the Day.* Illus. Sara Steele. San Diego: Lura Media, 1994.

Fitzjohn, Sue, Judy Large and Weston. *Festivals Together: A Guide to Multi-Cultural Celebration.* Stroud: Hawthorn Press, 1993.

Hanh, Thich Nhat and friends. *A Joyful Path: Community, Transformation and Peace.* Berkeley, CA: Parallax Press, 1994.

Johnson, Cait and Maura D. Shaw. *Celebrating the Great Mother: A Handbook of Earth-Honoring Activities for Parents and Children.* Rochester, VT: Destiny Books, 1995.

Johnson, Philip E. *More Celebrating the Seasons with Children.* Cleveland: Pilgrim Press, 1985.

Kelly, Armandine. *Seasonal Stories for Family Festivals.* San Jose: Resource Publications, 1987.

Kennedy, Marge. *100 Things You Can Do To Keep Your Family Together... when it sometimes seems like the whole world is trying to pull it apart.* Princeton, NJ: Peterson's, 1994.

Lieberman, Susan Able. *New Traditions: Redefining Celebrations for Today's Family.* Rev. ed. of *Let's Celebrate.* New York: Noonday Press, 1991.

Margolis, Vivienne, Kerry Smith and Adelle Weiss. *Fanfare for a Feather: 77 Ways to Celebrate Practically Anything.* San Jose: Resource Publications, 1991.

Moore, Robin. *Awakening the Hidden Storyteller: How to Build a Storytelling Tradition in Your Family.* Boston, Shambhala, 1991.

Patrick, Diane. *Family Celebrations.* Illus. Michael Bryant. Family Ties Series. New York: Silver Moon Press, 1993.

Powers, Mala. *Follow the Year: A Celebration of Family Holidays.* San Francisco: Harper & Row, 1985. *Christian celebrations and stories.*

Scott, Anne. *Serving Fire: Food for Thought, Body and Soul.* Berkeley: Celestial Arts, 1994.

Sheehan, Kathryn and Mary Waidner. *Earth Child: Games, Stories, Activities, Experiments & Ideas about Living Lightly on Planet Earth.* Rev. ed. Tulsa, OK: Council Oak Books, 1994.

Stillman, Peter. *Families Writing.* Cincinnati, OH: Writer's Digest Books, 1992.

Tudor, Tasha. *A Time To Keep: The Tasha Tudor Book of Holidays.* New York: Simon & Schuster, 1990.

Blessings for meals:

Kelly, Marcia and Jack. Calligraphy by Christopher Causby. *One Hundred Graces: Mealtime Blessings.* New York: Bell Tower/Crown Publishers, 1992.

Ryan, M. J., ed. *A Grateful Heart: Daily Blessings for the Evening Meal from Buddha to the Beatles.* Berkeley: Conari Press, 1994.

Stories to share as a family/community:

Allison, Christine, ed. *Teach Your Children Well: A Parent's Guide to the Stories, Poems, Fables and Tales that Instill Traditional Values.* New York: Delacorte Press, 1993.

Brody, Goldspinner, Green, Leventhal & Porcino, eds. *Spinning Tales, Weaving Hope: Stories of Peace, Justice and the Environment.* Illus. Lahri Bond. Philadelphia: New Society Publishers, 1992.

Feldman, Christina and Jack Kornfield. *Stories of the Spirit, Stories of the Heart: Parables of the Spiritual Path from Around the World.* San Francisco: Harper San Francisco, 1991.

Forest, Heather. *Wonder Tales from Around the World.* Little Rock, AK: August House Publishers, 1995.

Hamilton, Virginia. *Her Stories. African American Folktales, Fairy Tales and True Tales.* Illus. Leo & Diane Dillon. New York: Scholastic/Blue Sky, 1995.

Martin, Rafe. *One Hand Clapping: Zen Stories for All Ages.* Illus. Junko Morimoto. New York: Rizzoli, 1995.

Phelps, Ethel Johnson, ed. *Tatterhood and Other Tales.* Illus. Pamela Baldwin-Ford. Old Westbury, NY: Feminist Press, 1978. *Collection of folk and fairy tales with girls and women in courageous roles.*

Stillman, Peter. *Families Writing.* Cincinnati, OH: Writer's Digest Books, 1992.

85

The Adventure of Human Awareness

Approach history as a living process.
Cultivate empathy for the human experience.
Appreciate the abundance of wisdom held within each human life.
Listen to the stories, sing the songs, dance the dances, honor the wisdom of our collective experience.

*I*n a curriculum of spirit, history is best understood as a living process. When we begin to give our children an appreciation of the past not as a set of scattered facts or disconnected ideas, but as an ongoing thread in the tapestry of our lives, then the richness of past experience is appreciated and respected.

Perhaps we need a new language to describe this process of human cultural evolution as an ongoing continuum. Life cycles of cultural patterns live within us, not stored as facts, but integrated into the framework of our human wholeness.

When we show children a historical perspective by listening to people's stories, delving into the sounds and symbols of ancient and contemporary cultures through music, art, myths, language and imagination, we rekindle the flame of our awareness of the past. In this way, the study of history is not separate from our children's experience, but integral to their understanding of self as part of a collective human family.

If one acknowledges that our concept of time is limited, then the concept of history as memorized events becomes irrelevant. Integrating the experience and wisdom of the past with our visions for the future enhances children's appreciation of a vital collective past.

We can encourage children to understand our human experience not through memorization, but through participation. By exposing children to the real and imagined stories, songs, food and dances of people who have lived with vastly different life conditions than their own, they begin to experience the feeling of different times and cultures through their own bodies.

Encouraging children to feel empathy for the diversity of human expression offers them a path toward becoming compassionate adults. From this perspective, history and the learning of history means becoming conscious of ourselves in relation to the changing world, and to the peoples of the world. We provide our children with an opportunity to look back not by studying separate pieces of facts and events but as a process of discovery and adventure. We give them specific and imaginative ways to help them discover what past experiences can mean to them personally, and what lessons they offer us in the present.

Cultures and civilizations of the past are living patterns, still accessible through our physical bodies and imaginations. Children can re-experience and reconnect with past cultures by hearing ancient sounds, listening to the stories, sensing the energies in historic and sacred places. The past is stored within the wisdom of the body's memory, connecting us to the human experience as a vital living process, ever changing, ever forming.

The following activities encourage older children to experience the wisdom of the past through their own bodies and imaginations. Please refer to Resources at the end of this chapter for books appropriate for young children which encourage empathy for different life experiences.

LISTENING TO THE LIVING PAST THROUGH NATURE – Ages 8 and up

In these experiences "listening" is a whole body process which involves breathing, smelling, touching, sensing, feeling and intuiting.

YOU WILL NEED to find an elder tree, rock formation or similar place to bring children. You will also need journals, paper, writing tools and/or drawing supplies for writing things down.

DISCUSSION: *Nature is a wondrous teacher of history, development and transformation. Anyone who has looked at the rings inside the trunk of a tree is struck by a sense of awe at the process of growth and change we are all part of.*

There are many elders in nature ready to teach us some wisdom from their years upon this planet, if we are willing to listen.

Have each person find a special place with an elder rock, tree or other natural element. Give each child an opportunity to find a way to sit quietly with the experience and wisdom of this place.

Just relax in the space and allow your whole body to listen. What does it feel like being here? What kinds of smells, sensa-tions, feelings do you experience when you are here? Is there anything this tree (rock, place, etc.) would like to tell you about itself?

After some time (about five to ten minutes at least), ask the children to listen to this noble teacher for any stories it might have to tell about what it has seen, heard or felt. *Is there a message for you?*

Children can write, draw or just tell the stories they have heard. Have children begin to write in the first person, *"I am Tree… I have been in this place a long time…"*

They can choose to draw pictures of things this wise being has seen.

Note: You can bring nature into a room for a population that may not be able to travel. A stone, shell, small branch, can be given to someone to hold and listen to.

LISTENING TO LIVING HISTORY:
FAMILY STORIES AND ORAL TRADITIONS

Stories are the heart of a people. They are pathways of the soul. Telling stories is a process of going into the realm of spirit, and emerging transformed, with a deeper understanding of some road on the human experience which we all share.

Sharing our own stories with our children enables us to give our personal histories a meaning, and gives children access to that shared experience which makes them know themselves as more than single individuals, but as part of a community of seekers.

Any topic can be the basis for a story. Stories can be used to share values, explain the way things were, teach a lesson or simply entertain. There is no special skill needed to begin a tale, just a willingness to share an experience relevant to the listener.

As parents and teachers, we can look for the stories in our lives which can help illuminate some aspect of our children's current reality. In this way, the past becomes a bridge to the present and future.

ORAL BIOGRAPHIES AS LIVING HISTORY

Children can become researchers into the past by interviewing grand-parents, relatives, extended family members, community friends.

In a more informal way, letting younger children spend time with elder relatives and friends and listen to their stories can create a rich tapestry of living history.

LIFE STORY INTERVIEW – Ages 8 to adult; younger children with assistance

YOU WILL NEED: a willing elder, grandparent or friend. Determine time and quiet place for the interview. Tape recorder and tape (if kids are older or interested, you may use a home video-camera if available), notebook for questions.

You can choose to invite someone to come and speak with a group of children about their life stories, with different children asking questions, or arrange for children to conduct individual interviews at home with their chosen elder.

Here are some questions which may open the doorway to stories of the past:

–When and where were you born?

–Who were your parents? Where did they come from? What do you remember most about them?

– What's your earliest memory?

–Where did you live as a child, and what places do you most remember? What were your favorite places?

–What kinds of things did you do by yourself, with your family, with your friends?

–What kinds of foods did you eat? What were your favorite meals? Who did the cooking? How did your family celebrate holidays?

—*Who were your favorite people? Who were the people you most admired?*

—*What did you wear? How did you get around?*

—*How was life different from the way it is now?*

—*Do you have any favorite stories about your family?*

—*What values do you think are important for people to live by?*

FEELING HOW THINGS WERE: CREATIVE CONTEMPLATION

— Ages 6 and up

Imaginary journeys are a wonderful way for children to explore any kind of landscape without the limitations of time and space. Children can fly with their imaginations to many lands, many cultures and environments, having the opportunity to freely explore places and meet people who may no longer exist, except in the imagination.

Using guided imagery, children can utilize the creative potential of their whole brain and focus attention on a particular place, culture or time.

The following guided imagery journey can be adapted to travel to any specific time or place you may want children to explore.

TIME TRAVEL ADVENTURE: THE EARLIEST AMERICANS – Ages 8 and up

YOU WILL NEED: a quiet, peaceful space where the children can relax, either sitting on chairs or lying on a rug on the floor. The teacher can read the guided journey as children follow along in their imaginations. Journals, paper, writing and drawing tools for capturing the journey on paper afterwards.

Begin by letting children stretch, shake out and yawn with their whole bodies to loosen up and relax. (See Chapter One for exercises to integrate body, mind and breath.)

Take a deep breath and as you exhale, relax and release any tension and let go. Close your eyes, and take another deep breath. As you exhale, feel your body relax even more, settling comfortably in your chair or on the floor.

We're going to go on a journey in our imaginations. In order to take this journey, our bodies have to be very quiet and relaxed. We're going to help our bodies relax now by tightening our muscles and then letting all our muscles be relaxed and loose.

Now start by tightening all the muscles in your arms and hands. Squeeze your hands into fists, tighten your arms and shoulders... hold it tight... tighter... now, relax and let everything go.

Now tighten the muscles of your chest, back and belly... breathe in and squeeze all the muscles tight... tighter... now breathe out and relax. Take a deep breath in, and just let everything go as you breathe out.

Now tighten all the muscles of your legs and feet. Curl up your toes,

tighten your knees and thighs, hold… now breathe out and relax. Wiggle your toes, jiggle your legs a bit and just rest.

Now tighten all the muscles of your face, squeeze it into a little raisin shape around your nose and hold it there… now open your mouth and make your face really wide… wider… now just relax.

Your body feels loose and relaxed now, like a rag doll, and your muscles are as loose as cooked spaghetti. Your breathing is easy and relaxed.

You are about to take a journey back in time to a place long ago… In order to get there, you are going to create a vehicle that can travel through time and space. Imagine you are a great inventor and you are now inventing a very special travel craft. This craft can travel through time backwards or forwards. You can imagine your time travel vehicle is made any way you want it to be, and you know just how to use all the controls or ways it works.

Get into your vehicle and program it to travel back in time to when the earliest people lived on the continent of North America. Now blast off and you move swiftly through the speed of light…

You land, get out and look around. You see a vast continent, with great mountains, ice and snow. You see wild musk-oxen, mammoths, wild horses. There are plains and rivers, mountain sheep and beavers.

You notice smoke rising and smell a small fire. Around the fire are people wearing furs and skins of animals. There is a tent-like hut made of mammoth bones, covered with furs, and held in place by stones all around the bottom.

You see someone making a tool out of stone and bone. There is the smell of something good to eat roasting in the fire.

Now you will have some time to explore this world and the people there. Maybe there is someone or some animal you can communicate with. Let them show you whatever you need to know about this place and its people. (Allow a few minutes of silence.)

It's time now to return to this room and time. Say good-bye to your friends, thank them and let them know you can return again. Allow them to give you something to bring back with you.

Back into your time craft, set the controls to bring you back home. Whoosh… through the speed of light you return to this room. When you open your eyes you'll be able to remember everything about your journey. I'm going to count backwards from 10 to 1, and by the time I reach 1, you'll be back in our room with your eyes open. 10…9…8…7…6…5…4…3…2…1.

Now open your eyes!

Distribute paper or journals and let children draw pictures of their time machine and what they saw. Have them write down what the gift was, or anything they want to remember from their time journey.

FEELING EMPATHY: STORIES THAT OPEN DOORS – Ages 4 and up

Stories and picture books provide a way for children to experience the feeling of growing up at different times in the evolution of human experience.

You may wish to use some of the books listed in Resources at the end of this chapter to elicit a feeling for the way people have lived throughout different times and places.

After reading the stories, share ideas with children about what it would have felt like to live at these different times. Have the children draw pictures of themselves living in a different time or place, as suggested by the stories.

SIX: The Adventure of Human Awareness

Illustrated books for children which cultivate empathy for growing up in different times and cultures:
Ages 4–8

Anno, Mitsumasa. *Anno's Journey.* New York: Putnam Publishing, 1981. *A travel journey by boat from Japan to America.*

Bartone, Elise. *Peppe the Lamplighter.* New York: Lothrop, Lee & Shepard Books, 1993. *An Italian-American immigrant boy helps his family.*

Brett, Jan. *The First Dog.* New York: Harcourt Brace Jovanovich, 1988. *During the Pleistocene, Kip the cave boy names Paleowolf the first dog.*

Bunting, Eve. *How Many Days to America? A Thanksgiving Story.* Illus. Beth Peck. New York: Clarion Books, 1988. *Refugees from a Caribbean island journey to America.*

Cooney, Barbara. *Island Boy.* New York: Viking Kestrel, 1988.

Cooney, Barbara. *Miss Rumphius.* New York: Puffin Books/Viking Penguin, 1982.

First Start Biographies. *Famous People: Famous Lives.* Mahwah, NJ: Troll Associates.

Gilman, Phoebe. *Something from Nothing.* New York: Scholastic, Inc., 1993. *Adapted from a traditional Jewish folktale with an old world village setting.*

Heide, Florence Perry and Judith Heide Gilliland. *The Day of Ahmed's Secret*. Illus. by Ted Lewin. New York: Lothrop, 1991. *A young boy's accomplishment is shared with family after a busy day in Cairo.*

Hall, Donald. *Ox-Cart Man*. Illus. Barbara Cooney. Harmondsworth: Penguin, 1983. *Early 19th-century New England family life through the seasons.*

Levinson, Nancy Smiler. *Clara and the Bookwagon*. Illus. Carolyn Croll. New York: Harper Collins Children's Books, 1988.

Medicine Story. *The Children of the Morning Light: Wampanoag Tales as told by Manitonguat*. Illus. Mary F. Arquette. New York: Macmillan, 1994.

Pogrebin, Letty C. "My Grandma" in *Free to Be... a Family*. Marlo Thomas and Friends. New York: Bantam Books, 1987.

Pryor, Bonnie. *The House on Maple Street*. Illus. Beth Peck. New York: Mulberry/William Morrow, Inc., 1987. *A journey through the 300 years of occupants of the place that is now a house on Maple Street.*

Rylant, Cynthia. *When I Was Young in the Mountains*. Unicorn Paperbacks Series. New York: Dutton, 1982.

Shelby, Anne. *Homeplace*. Illus. Wendy Halperin. New York: Orchard Books, 1995. *A story of generations and profound changes as told from grandmother to granddaughter.*

Spierer, Peter. *People*. New York: Doubleday, 1988.

Whiteley, Opal. *Only Opal: The Diary of a Young Girl*. Illus. Barbara Cooney. New York: Scholastic, Inc., 1995. *A girl's diary from Oregon in the early 1900's.*

Ages 8 and up

Cobblestone: The History Magazine for Young People; Faces: The Magazine About People; Calliope: The Magazine About World History, Petersborough, NH: Cobblestone Publishing, 7 School Street, Petersborough, NH 03458, (800) 821-0115.

Foreman, Michael. *The Boy Who Sailed with Columbus*. New York: Arcade, 1992.

Nolan, Dennis. *Wolf Child*. New York: Macmillan, 1989. *An adventure set 18,000 years ago, when people and animals first became companions.*

Reynolds, Jan. *Vanishing Cultures Series*. The series includes the books, *Mongolia, Amazon Basin* and *Far North*. New York: Harcourt Brace Jovanovich, 1992–1994.

Waters, Kate. *Sarah Morton's Day: A Day in the Life of a Pilgrim Girl*. New York: Scholastic, Inc., 1989.

Young adults

Berry, James. *Ajeemah and His Son*. New York: William Pulman Books/Harper Collins Books, 1994.

Blake, Noah. *Diary of an Early American Boy, Noah Blake, 1805*. ed. Eric Sloane. New York: Ballantine Books, 1974.

Filipovic, Zlata. *Zlata's Diary: A Child's Life in Sarajevo*. New York: Viking, 1994.

Frank, Anne. *Anne Frank: The Diary of a Young Girl*. Reprint. New York: Bantam Books, 1993.

Stewart, Elinore Pruitt. *Letters of a Woman Homesteader*. Reprint. Boston: Houghton Mifflin, 1982.

Storm, Hyemeyohsts. *Seven Arrows*. New York: Ballantine Books, 1985.

Reference:

Maestro, Betsy and Giulio. *The Discovery of the Americas: From Prehistory through the Age of Columbus.* New York: Mulberry/ William Morrow, 1991.

Perl, Lila. *It Happened in America: True Stories from the Fifty States.* New York, Henry Holt, 1992.

Reader's Digest Books. *Everyday Life Through the Ages, 1992.*

Sattler, Helen Roney. *The Earliest Americans.* New York: Clarion Books, 1993. *Paleo Indians through the 1400's.*

Wood, Jenny. *The Children's Atlas of People and Places.* Brookfield, CT: Millbrook Press, 1993.

Music, songs and audio collections:

✿ *indicates sound cassette or recording*
△ *indicates printed songbook collection*

△ Blood, Peter and Annie Patterson, *Rise Up Singing Songbook. The Group Singing Songbook.* Rev. ed. Bethlehem, PA: Sing-Out! Publications, 1992.

△ Cohen, Amy L., ed. Illus. by Caldicott Medalists. *From Sea To Shining Sea: A Treasury of American Folktales and Folk Songs.* New York: Scholastic, 1993.

✿ "Like Me Like You." Raffi. *One Light One Sun.* MCA Records, 1985.

△ Mattox, Cheryl Warren. Illus. by Varnette P. Honeywood. *Shake It To the One You Love Best: Play Songs and Lullabies from the Black Musical Traditions.* Warren-Mattox Productions, 1991.

✿ Pelham, Ruth. *Under One Sky.* A Gentle Wind, 1982.

✿ *Sing Children Sing* series. Songs from Austria, Congo, France, Italy, Israel, Mexico, British Isles. Caedmon Records.

❀ *Tales of the Desert. Tales of the Hopi. Tales of China & Tibet.* Caedmon Records.

❀ "Walk a Mile." Vitamin L. *Walk a Mile.* Loveable Creature Music, 1989.

❀ "We All Sing with the Same Voice." Monet, Lisa. *My Best Friend.* Music for Little People, 1991.

❀ *Wee Sing Around the World.* Price Stern Sloan, 1994.

Telling the family stories:

Colgin, Mary L. and Thea S. Van Der Ven. *It's Your Story — Pass It On.* Manlius, NY: Colgin Publishing, 1986.

Lord, Frank K. *Stories They'll Remember: Teaching Children Values through Stories from Your Experience.* Loveland, OH: Treehaus Communications, 1987.

Stillman, Peter. *Families Writing.* Cincinnati, OH: Writer's Digest Books, 1992.

Wakefield, Dan. *The Story of Your Life: Writing a Spiritual Autobiography.* Boston: Beacon Press, 1990.

Zimmerman, William. *How To Tape Instant Oral Biographies.* Illus. Tom Bloom. Rev. ed. New York: Guarionex Press, Ltd., 1994.

Books on guided imagery and visualization:

Garth, Maureen. "The Grandfather Tree" in *Starbright: Meditations for Children.* San Francisco: Harper San Francisco, 1991.

Garth, Maureen. *The Inner Garden: Meditations for Life from 9 to 90.* North Blackburn, Vic.: Collins Dove, 1994.

Garth, Maureen. Sunshine. *More Meditations for Children*. San Francisco, CA: Harper Collins, 1995.

"Magic Carpet Ride." in Capacchione, Lucia. *The Creative Journal for Children: A Guide for Parents, Teachers and Counselors*. Boston, MA: Shambhala, 1989.

Murdock, Maureen. *Spinning Inward: Using Guided Imagery with Children for Learning, Creativity and Relaxation*. Boston, MA: Shambhala, 1987.

Zimmerman, Bill. *Make Beliefs: A Way to Fool Around and Explore New Possibilities*. New York: Bantam Books, 1992.

Audio tapes for guided imagery:

MindWorks for Children: Guided Relaxation and Imagery Journeys. Daleo, Roxanne. P.O. Box 2493, Cambridge, MA 02238.

Supporting Your Child's Inner Life: Guided Visualizations for Children. Ananda School – Education for Life Foundation. 14618 Tyler Foote Road, Nevada City, CA 95959.

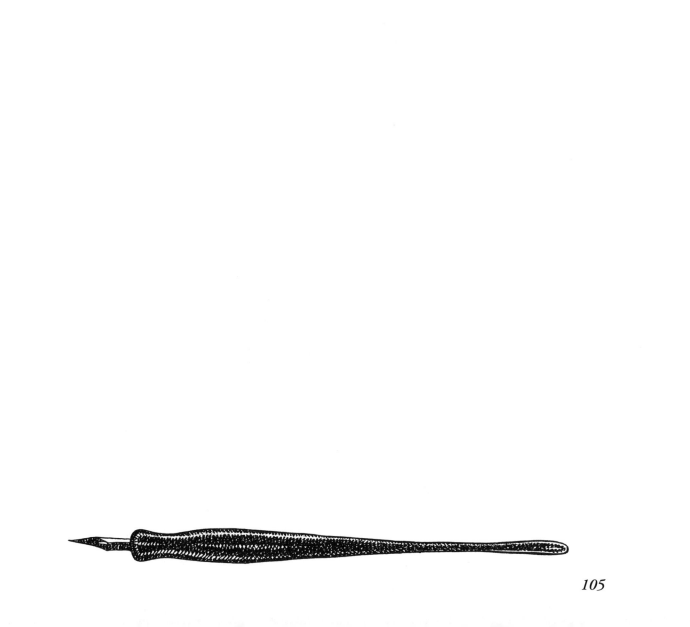

Nourishing Compassion

Practice seeing with the heart.
Acknowledge the best in one another.
Work together with kindness and forgiveness.

How do we teach our children compassion? We teach what we need to learn. This is certainly true in the teaching of compassion.

What is compassion? First, it is the willingness to open our hearts to one another. We look at pain, joy, indeed all life experiences with an open heart and mind. We try to understand the needs of others, and do something useful for one another.

We can encourage children to remember that being compassionate is not about pitying one another or judging another person's circumstances. It is a practice of looking at each living being, and as we look, seeing tremendous potential within. Compassion is seeing with the heart, looking at our sisters and brothers as part of one human family. Compassion is the true unifying principle in our human journey.

Although compassion is an inner action of the heart, we practice compassion through our outer actions. Empathy, kind actions and forgiveness are the doorways to this path. To teach compassion we show children how we make ourselves useful in the world, spreading kindness and hope. This is a lesson we really cannot share through words alone, for children model not

what we talk about, but what we do in our moment to moment experience.

We teach compassion when we help one another in our families, neighborhoods and communities. We begin to encourage an awareness of family that extends beyond relatives, and includes the wider circle of humanity.

Demonstrating the many ways people can help one another may bring up difficult, indeed even catastrophic, events that occur in people's lives. It may seem inappropriate to bring up "bad" news with young children. Surrounding young children with positive images and loving environments is a natural and necessary desire. However, children are extremely perceptive, and by the time they are six and seven, they have begun to realize that many people need help, and that the world is much less predictable than they had once imagined.

Doing something for others in the midst of crisis or need is the first step toward letting children understand that hardships bring opportunities to practice loving kindness. There are always angels among us, and each one of us has the capacity to minister help where it is needed.

DEVELOPING EMPATHY: UNDERSTANDING THE NEEDS OF OTHERS

Collect stories of people offering hope and help in times of crisis: rescue stories, help to victims of natural disasters, community reports of rescues, etc.

At the time of the devastating Oklahoma bombing in which many families lost children and loved ones, many community groups in our local area organized a letter writing campaign from our children to the Oklahoma families.

In their letters, the children drew pictures, and offered words of hope and consolation for the bereaved families. In times of crisis, letters and drawings can always be sent to a Mayor or town clerk's office or to a local newspaper.

DISCUSSION: Choose a recent event in which children and families were in need of assistance. Ask children: *How would you feel if you were in this situation?*

What do you think the people in this situation need?

Is there anything you can imagine doing to help?

Invite children to imagine ways of offering assistance. Can any of these ideas be implemented?

MEETING PEOPLE WHO TAKE ACTION

Find someone in your community who is involved in taking steps to better the world for others: local Red Cross, volunteer firefighters, Hunger Relief, etc. Invite them to come and share their experiences with your group.

You can also take children out into the community to look for ways people are involved in helping others and showing they care.

MODELS OF COMPASSION – Ages 6 and up

Learning about people who have devoted themselves to the good of others is an important step in recognizing the work we can do on earth. Share stories about the compassion and passion of the great teachers, Moses, Jesus, the Buddha. Share stories of contemporary teachers, Ghandi, Martin Luther King, Jr., Mother Theresa. Look for people whose lives have changed the lives of many others, like Clara Barton, Harriet Tubman, George Washington Carver, Sequoyah and many others. *See Resources.*

COMPASSION AND FORGIVENESS

It is sometimes easier for us to have compassion for strangers than to let go of our judgments of those closest to us.

Our children need to see the path of love and forgiveness working in our own lives. When we function from love and understanding, rather than reaction, fear and judgment, then we will be honest in our effort to teach compassion.

When a child is caught in anger and blame, we can gently remind them to take the time to breathe deeply, relax the body, sit quietly for a moment. They may not be able to control the situation which upsets them, but they can control their response to it.

There are many ways you can encourage forgiveness. The first step is to help your child calm down, and try to see a situation of conflict as an opportunity to practice letting go of fear and blame.

NOURISHING THE SEEDS OF COMPASSION

Seeing with the heart is a process which takes practice and willingness. One path to nourishing the seeds of compassion in our children is to encourage them to unclutter their speedy minds and slow down. We can not really help another if we ourselves are full of worries, fear, tensions and judgments.

Prayer, contemplative listening, guided imagery, relaxation and silence all work to clear the mind, calm the body and encourage a sense of peace which can allow for the seeds of compassion to take root.

In their imaginations, children can meet God in whatever form God speaks to them, talk to angels, fly across the world to bring love and flowers of peace where they are needed. The limitations of time and space disappear in the realm of prayer and holy contemplation.

PRACTICING FORGIVENESS: A GUIDED IMAGINARY JOURNEY

– Ages 10 and older

Note: This exercise is meant to deal with ordinary occurrences of upsetting events common in a child's life. In cases of serious abuse or deep-rooted conflict, there may be need for professional help and a commitment to the practice of forgiveness which is beyond the scope of this curriculum.

YOU WILL NEED: a quiet, peaceful environment in which children can sit on chairs or lie on the floor with their eyes closed.

Take a moment to stretch out your body, take a big yawn, and as you breathe out, just relax, let all tension release. Now sit comfortably, rest your body and with your eyes closed, take another deep breath and relax even further.

Imagine you have the ability to, with your eyes closed, see inside someone else, looking past their actions, looking past what they look like from the outside, to seeing them for who they truly are, beautiful, whole children of God (light, love, Spirit, whatever word seems right to you).

You might imagine seeing a bright, shining heart radiating inside the body of the person you are envisioning.

Now imagine you can look inside anyone and see this radiant heart, the beautiful inner light trying to shine through to the outside world. You can see each different person in your family in this way: mother, father, brother, sister, grandparent.

Now remember a time recently when someone very close to you did something, and in response you became angry or hurt. See the person you feel angry with... imagine as you look at them you can begin to see through the outside face they are showing you, to the place inside their heart which is pure.

Just notice what begins to happen to your anger when you focus on their inner beauty. Let the feelings of anger or hurt begin to melt, to soften as you watch their light trying to shine through.

See yourself extend your hand to them, and see a bridge of light stream from your hand to their hand... when the bridge meets, imagine your heart shines pure and strong as well.

Look into their eyes and see the eyes of a very wise being looking out at you from within them.

If you want to, you can envision being able to hug the person, feeling a sense of inner calm as you do.

Now when you feel ready, slowly open your eyes and come back to the room.

After this visualization, you may want to draw a picture of what you imagined. Make sure you put yourself in the picture, too.

The Resources included at the end of this chapter reinforce the understanding that peace begins within.

SEVEN: Nourishing Compassion

Illustrated books for children which encourage listening with the heart:

Baylor, Byrd. *The Other Way To Listen*. Illus. Peter Parnall. New York: Charles Scribner's Sons, 1978.

Bliss, Corinne D. *Matthew's Meadow*. Illus. Ted Lewin. New York: Harcourt Brace Jovanovich, 1992.

Fyleman, Rose. *A Fairy Went A-Marketing*. New York: Dutton, 1986.

Parnall, Peter. *Quiet*. Morrow Junior Books. New York: William Morrow & Co., 1989.

Tapes:

Daleo, Roxanne. *"The Healing Heart"* Guided Imagery and Relaxation Journeys, MindWorks for Children, P.O. Box 2493, Cambridge, MA 02238-2493.

Books for children which encourage the values of compassion and service:
Ages 7 and up

Armstrong, Carole. *Lives and Legends of the Saints: with Paintings from the Great Art Museums of the World*. New York: Simon & Schuster, 1995.

Boelts, Maribeth and Darwin Boelts. *Kids To the Rescue! First Aid Techniques for Kids*. Illus. Marina Megale. Seattle, WA: Parenting Press, 1992.

Brown, Fern. *Special Olympics*. First Books. New York: Franklin Watts, 1992.

Coerr, Eleanor. *Sadako and the Thousand Paper Cranes*. New York: Putnam, 1977.

Giff, Patricia Reilly. *Mother Teresa: Sister to the Poor*. Illus. Ted Lewin. New York: Puffin Books, 1987.

Great Achievers. Lives of the Physically Challenged Series. New York: Chelsea House Publishers, 1993–1996.

Jakata Tales for Children: 12 Asian Folktales for Grades 1 - 6 with Teacher Resource Guide. Berkeley, CA: Dharma Publishing, 2910 San Pablo Ave, Berkeley, CA 94702, (800) 873-4276. *Tales of heroic animals and human beings whose wise and compassionate actions transform obstacles, foster courage, caring, cooperation, unselfishness and other core values.*

Junior World Biographies. Series includes *Nelson Mandela, Eleanor Roosevelt, Harriet Tubman* and many others. New York: Chelsea Juniors, 1991–1996.

Kibbey, Marsha. *The Helping Place*. Illus. Jennifer Hagerman. Minneapolis, MN: Carolrhoda Books, Inc., 1991.

Lewis, Shari. *One-Minute Great Americans*. Series includes *Clara Barton, Helen Keller, Martin Luther King, Jr.* and many others. New York: Doubleday, 1990.

Marzollo, Jean. *My First Book of Biographies: Great Men and Women Every Child Should Know*. Illus. Irene Trivas. Includes "Mohandas Gandhi," "Hokusai," "Cesar Chavez" and many others. New York: Scholastic, Inc., 1994.

Moore, Eva. *The Story of George Washington Carver*. New York: Scholastic, Inc., 1971.

Osofsky, Audrey. *My Buddy*. Illus. Ted Rand. New York: Henry Holt & Co., 1992. *How a dog helps a young physically challenged boy.*

Shea, George. *Amazing Rescues*. Illus. Marshall H. Peck. *Step Into Reading Books for grades 2–3*. New York: Random House, 1992.

Versfeld, Ruth. *Why are People Hungry?* New York: Gloucester Press, 1988.

Nourishing Compassion

Songs and music:

✿ "That Quiet Place" and "There's Always Something You Can Do." Pirtle, Sarah. *Two Hands Hold The Earth*. A Gentle Wind, 1984.

✿ "What Can One Little Person Do?" Rogers, Sally. *What Can One Little Person Do?* Round River Records, 1992.

✿ "What Do I Do?" Pelham, Ruth. *Under One Sky*. A Gentle Wind, 1982.

Children cultivating compassion:

Conari Press Editors. *Kids' Random Acts of Kindness*. Berkeley: Conari Press, 1994.

Lewis, Barbara A. *A Kid's Guide to Service Projects: Over 500 Service Ideas for Young People Who Want to Make a Difference*. Minneapolis, MN: Free Spirit Publishing, Inc., 1995.

Books for adults:

Boone, J. Allen. *Kinship with All Life*. New York: Harper, 1954. *The universal language of love as spoken between animals and humans.*

Casarjian, Robin. *Forgiveness: A Bold Choice for a Peaceful Heart*. New York: Bantam Books, 1992.

Conari Press, ed. *The Practice of Kindness: Meditations for Bringing More Simplicity, Love and Compassion into Daily Life*. Berkeley, CA: Conari Press, 1996.

A Course in Miracles. Glen Ellen, CA: Foundation for Inner Peace, 1976, 1996.

The Dalai Lama with Daniel Goleman, Stephen Levine, Jean Shinoda Bolen, Daniel Brown, Jack Engler, Margaret Brenman-Gibson and Joanna Macy. *Worlds in Harmony: Dialogues on Compassionate Action*. Berkeley, CA: Parallax Press, P.O. Box 7355, Berkeley, CA 94707, (510) 525-0101.

Dass, Ram and Paul Gorman. *How Can I Help? Stories and Reflections on Service*. New York: Alfred A. Knopf, 1985.

Ingram, Catherine. *In The Footsteps of Gandhi: Conversations with Spiritual Social Activists*. Berkeley: Parallax Press, 1990.

Nhat Hanh, Thich. *Being Peace*. Berkeley: Parallax Press, 1987.

Nhat Hanh, Thich. *Living Buddha. Living Christ*. New York: Riverhead, 1995.

Reynolds, Rebecca A. *Bring Me the Ocean: Nature as Teacher, Messenger and Intermediary*. Acton, MA: VanderWyk & Burnham Publishing Co., 1995. *How animals and nature can provide therapeutic assistance to those in need*.

Salzberg, Sharon. *Lovingkindness: The Revolutionary Art of Happiness*. Boston: Shambhala Publications, 1995.

Singh, Tara. *Awakening a Child from Within*. Los Angeles: Life Action Press, 1991.

118

Appreciating Beauty

Cultivate beauty.
Let color, shape and texture
show the glory of Divine order,
Divine harmony.

A child has an innate appreciation of beauty. It is natural for children to seek order, to thrive on rhythm. This search for ordering the universe creates harmony throughout life.

In cultivating beauty with children the primary consideration is to nourish the expression of beauty from within the soul of the child rather than impose an outer definition of beauty.

Color is a primary factor in developing an aesthetic and kinesthetic sensitivity to beauty. Be aware of the colors that surround a child. The color of clothes, rooms in which a child works and plays, coverings on the walls—all these contribute to a certain quality of attention and state of mind.

Each age tends to gravitate toward certain colors, and radiate within particular color harmonies. Our role as caretakers is to strive to offer children a full color bath in their surroundings, by exposing them to the range of color nature offers.

When you walk with children, try to open their awareness to the colors surrounding them, simply by providing ways to interact with these natural elements: the blue of sky and sea, the brown of earth, tree trunks, limbs, green of a meadow, dancing leaves, red berries, black insects, pure white clouds.

Beauty is first learned by interacting with and appreciating the natural world, the larger rhythms of day and night, seasons and growth. A child encouraged to move freely in the natural world will certainly evolve a sense of aesthetic beauty and harmony.

Color, as expressed through art, is a primary movement of the soul's longing for union with universal harmony. Giving children an opportunity to immerse themselves in the making of art encourages a deep respect for the creative impulse, the pure joy of personal expression and a natural relationship with the order of the universe.

Children are natural artists; they love to manipulate materials for the sheer pleasure of the experience. For younger children, the goal needs to remain the process of exploration. Encouraging children to expand their choice of materials and range of expression, without becoming attached to any judgment of the final product, makes for the most positive experience.

The following activities encourage freedom of expression within the framework of cultivating aesthetic pleasure, and are appropriate for all ages.

TAKE A BEAUTY WALK

Let there be beauty before me as I wander
Let there be beauty behind me as I wander
Let there be beauty above and below me as I wander
Let these eyes see only beauty from this day on.

Native American blessing song

Gather children together and share with them the idea of walking outside to see how many colors, shapes, textures, they can discover. As you walk, have the group gather around different discoveries, appreciating brown pebbles and patches of earth, soft green leaves, sparkling white glimmers in the sidewalks, wet black streets, etc. Compare different shades of the same color, green stems, leaves, grass.

You can choose to make this walk be a "looking only" walk, or one in which the children can collect a few treasures to bring back for arrangements or art projects.

COLOR EXHIBIT

Start collecting various colors of found objects, both natural and man-made. Collect shades of brown, gray and white from twigs, stones, bark, leaves, pods, shells, feathers, etc. REMEMBER, only take things that have fallen, never strip bark from a tree.

Add items to your collection such as buttons, bits of paper and fabric, string, rubber bands, nuts, bolts, corks, old stamps, paper clips, etc.

Have children take turns arranging these items on a changing exhibit table or shelf. You can choose to use only natural items, or mix in other objects as well.

Save other objects not being used for display in shoe boxes for use in collages or sculpture projects.

FRUIT OR FLOWER FEST

If your area has a local orchard, fruit stand or vegetable market, take the children to appreciate the rows of beautifully colored fruit and vegetables. If possible, you can bring back some fruit for a seasonal festival of color: apples, pumpkins, squash, gourds, or in summer: blueberries, strawberries, watermelon, red and green peppers. You can include fruit grown in other parts of the country or world: bananas, kiwi, mangoes, etc.

Let children take turns arranging fruit in a bowl, or spreading the items out on a table.

If gathering fruit to bring back is not possible, just letting kids absorb the colors in the fruit and vegetable section of a supermarket will give them a great color bath.

EAT YOUR COLORS!

Preparing a fruit salad with one piece of fruit from each child can also be a great way to begin thinking and feeling good about color, and to appreciate the beauty and bounty of earth's blessings.

LET BEAUTY BLOOM

Allow children to explore all the colors of the flowers: petals, stem, leaves, pistil, etc. You can start an indoor flower garden, planting flowers based on their colors and beauty. Bringing in a bouquet of wild or cut flowers also enhances the spirit of a room.

Let your children talk to the nature spirits, fairies and devas of the flowers and plants, asking permission before you take any cuttings, and always leaving a blessing of thanks in return.

If your area has a botanical garden, flower or herb garden, take the children and let them immerse themselves in the lush plants and flowers.

EXPERIMENT WITH COLOR: WATERCOLOR WET ON WET

YOU WILL NEED: chunky child-sized paintbrushes, watercolor paper, tubes or pots of watercolor (red, yellow, blue), small containers for water, sponges, plastic mat or plastic table covering.

Younger children do very well with chunky brushes on large pieces of paper, especially letting them work wet on wet with one, single, primary color at a time.

With a wet sponge, wet both sides of a piece of watercolor paper, then flatten it out with your hand onto a plastic mat or vinyl table covering. Using one color on a brush, allow child to freely brush wet watercolor wash onto paper. Set aside to dry. Use only one color at a time.

Later, you can experiment with adding a second color to the first.

CRAYON RUBBINGS

YOU WILL NEED: chunky or flat crayons without any paper on them, white art paper to rub onto, doilies, flattened leaves or cut paper shapes to put under white paper, a large piece of newsprint or newspaper to cover table.

Arrange leaves, doilies or cut-out shapes on top of newsprint. Tape white paper over arrangement. With flat end of the crayon, rub over the items until shapes appear. Use one, two or more colored crayons.

WRITE AND ILLUSTRATE A COLOR POEM – Ages 7 and up

YOU WILL NEED: small sponges cut into different shapes, poster paints, small trays or jar tops for holding paint and dipping sponges into, sheets of sturdy art paper, *Hailstones and Halibut Bones*, a book of color poems by Mary O'Neill, markers or colored pencils.

Ask children to name their favorite color and to describe how different colors make them feel. List things of that color.

Start with a separate paper for each individual color. Use sponges to create bright borders of a single color all around the inside edges of the paper.

After paint is dried, write down images, feelings and things in that same color with markers or colored pencils in the middle of the paper. Words and pictures can work together inside the painted borders.

For more ideas and color poems read *Hailstones and Halibut Bones* by Mary O'Neill.

3-DIMENSIONAL SCULPTURE – Ages 6 and up

YOU WILL NEED: modeling clay or plasticene, found objects collected from inside and outside, resources of different shapes, textures and colors, colored construction paper.

Allow child to shape clay into any form. Begin to add, arrange and create with different colored objects placed into the base clay form. Display sculptures on brightly colored pieces of construction paper.

EIGHT: Appreciating Beauty

Illustrated books for young children cultivating an appreciation for beauty and art:

Collins, Pat Lowery. *I am an Artist*. Millbrook Press, 1992.

Jonas, Ann. *Color Dance*. New York: Greenwillow Books, 1989.

Rylant, Cynthia. *All I See*. Illus. Peter Catalanatto. New York: Orchard Books, 1994.

Samson, Suzanne. *Fairy Dusters and Blazing Stars: Exploring Wildflowers with Children*. Illus. Preston Neel. Niwot, CO: Roberts Rinehart Publishers, 1994.

Sasso, Sandy Eisenberg. *God's Paintbrush*. Illus. Annette C. Compton. Woodstock, VT: Jewish Lights Publishing, 1992.

Walsh, Ellen Stohl. *Mouse Paint*. New York: Harcourt Brace, 1969.

Ages 7 and up:

Beckett, Sister Wendy. *A Child's Book of Prayer in Art*. New York: Dorling Kindersley, 1995.

Famous Artists Series. Series includes *Cezanne, Da Vinci, Michelangelo, Van Gogh*. Hauppauge, NY: Barrons, 1993–1995.

Roalf, Peggy. *Looking at Paintings*. Series includes the books *Families, Children, Flowers*. New York: Hyperion Books, 1992–1994.

Sullivan, Charles, ed. *Here is My Kingdom: Hispanic-American Literature and Art for Young People.* New York: Harry N. Abrams, 1994.

Thomson, Ruth. *Get Set... GO!* Series includes the books *Drawing, Painting, Printing, Collage.* Chicago: Children's Press, 1994.

Turner, Robyn. *Portraits of Women Artists for Children.* Series includes the books *Mary Cassatt, Faith Ringgold, Rosa Bonheur.* Boston: Little, Brown & Co. 1991–1994.

Waters, Elizabeth and Annie Harris. *Painting: A Young Artist's Guide.* Royal Academy of Arts. New York: Dorling Kindersley, 1993. *A creative guide for young artists, including hands-on projects, and a gallery of paintings by known and contemporary painters.*

Poetry Collections:

Koch, Kenneth and Kate Farrel, eds. *Talking to The Sun: An Illustrated Anthology of Poems for Young People.* New York: Metropolitan Museum of Art, 1993.

O'Neill, Mary. *Hailstones and Halibut Bones: Adventures in Color.* Illus. Leonard Weisgard. New York: Doubleday, 1961.

Songs and music:

    ✿ *indicates sound cassette or recording*
    △ *indicates printed songbook collection*

✿ "De Colores." Pirtle, Sarah. *Two Hands Hold the Earth.* A Gentle Wind, 1985.

✿ "Evergreen, Everblue." Raffi. *Evergreen, Everblue.* MCA Records, 1990.

✿ "I Can Sing a Rainbow." Penner, Fred. *Happy Feet.* Oak Street Music, 1992.

✿ "I've Got the Blues, Greens and Reds." Chapin, Tom. *Billy the Squid.* Sony, 1992.

❀ "Keep it Green." Harley, Bill. *Big, Big World*. A & M Records, 1993.

❀ "Mixing Colors." Rosen, Gary. *Tot Rock*. Lightyear Records, 1993.

❀ "Put a Little Color on You." Palmer, Hap. *Can a Cherry Pie Wave Goodbye?* Hap-pal Music, 1991.

❀ "Rainbow Round Me." Pelham, Ruth. *Under One Sky*. A Gentle Wind, 1982.

❀ "See the Beauty." Vitamin L. *Everyone's Invited*. Loveable Creature Music, 1993.

Books for adults:

Brookes, Mona. *Drawing with Children: A Creative Teaching and Learning Method That Works for Adults, Too*. Los Angeles, CA: J. P. Tarcher, 1986.

Brookes, Mona. *Drawing for Older Children And Teens: A Creative Method for Adult Beginners, Too*. Los Angeles: J. P. Tarcher, 1991.

Carlson, Laurie. *EcoArt! Earth-Friendly Art & Craft Experiences for 3- to 9-Year-Olds*. Illus. Loretta T. Braren. Charlotte, VT: Williamson Publishing Co., 1993.

Kohl, MaryAnn F. *Pre-school Art: It's the Process, Not the Product*. Illus. K. Whelan Dery. Beltsville, MD: Gryphon House, 1994.

Kohl, MaryAnn F. *Scribble Art: Independent Creative Art Experiences for Children*. Illus. Judy McCoy. Bellingham, WA: Bright Ring Publishing, 1994.

Milord, Susan. *Adventures in Art: Art & Craft Experiences For 7- to 14-year-olds*. Charlotte, VT: Williamson Publishing, 1990.

Muller, Brunhild. *Painting With Children*. Edinburgh: Floris, 1987.

Topal, Cathy Weisman. *Children and Painting*. Worcester, MA: Davis Publications, 1992. *Teaching painting creatively with inspirational activities, and hundreds of children's and professional paintings.*

Developing Balance

Encourage children to live in balance.
Bring body, mind and emotions into harmony.
Learn to adapt to change
with flexibility and strength.

Balance is the wisdom of a stable mind, a steady vision, an open heart. Balance is a wholeness nourished by work and activity, fed by silence and stillness and encouraged by faith.

To be in balance is to walk firmly on the earth rooted in the present moment, with a flexible spine, free-flowing breath and an open heart. To live in balance is to respect relationships between self and planet, self and others, self and God.

It is essential to understand the concept of balance as a process of aligning body, breath, being. Developing balance is not about finding or maintaining a still point which is rigid or fixed. Rather, it is a continuum which involves actively sensing and adjusting the flow of movement through the body. Developing balance is learning to adapt to a constantly changing world with flexibility and ease.

To teach our children to live in balance, we can begin with the process of centering, bringing body, mind and spirit into alignment, which can be initiated through physical, mental and emotional centering.

APPROACHING BALANCE PHYSICALLY: DEVELOPING STABILITY
– Ages 6 and up

The following exercises enable children to develop the awareness of centering the body by allowing energy to flow harmoniously through the entire body from the center.

To initiate balance physically we can begin by developing an awareness of the body's physical center, the pelvic area as a hub of a wheel from which all else radiates.

FEEL THE BELLY

Ask children to stand comfortably in a circle, and have them put their hands on their bellies, at the point just below the navel. Explain how this area is the center of their bodies, like the hub of a wheel. It is their source of power and energy. In Yoga, this sacred center is called the "hara," in T'ai Chi it is called "Ta 'tien".

GETTING GROUNDED

Now have everyone stand firmly on their feet, with their legs just a bit wider than the pelvis.

Imagine there is a flow of energy from your center/belly down each leg, going deep into the earth. You are feeling a triangle with the point just below your navel, and the two sides right through your legs and feet.

WEIGHT SHIFT

Begin to sway slightly from side to side, shifting your weight from one foot to the other, and without lifting your feet from the ground, feel the connection from your belly down to the center of the earth. Each time you shift your weight, you feel the body's center, the pelvis, moving smoothly, while staying connected to the earth.

UPPER BODY/LOWER BODY: SIDE/SIDE BALANCE

Continue to shift your weight gently from side to side, and as you do, just let the arms push the air away from the body, from one side to the other.

Each time you shift right, the right arm pushes the air away from the center to the right, each time you shift left, the left arm pushes left.

SOUNDING FROM THE CENTER

Now allow the breath to flow from the belly out of your mouth; with each push, make a "SSHHH" sound.

After several of these weight shifts/pushes with sound, see what happens when you move your feet, so you are now shifting your weight more forwards and backwards, and then with the other foot forward, as you push the air away with your hands and arms, making sound as you go.

CHOPPING WOOD:
BODY AND BREATH IN BALANCE

Imagine you are going to chop a very big piece of wood which is just in front of you. As you inhale, you raise up your arms above your head, with palms together. Now, bring your arms down, as you bend your knees gently to chop the wood. Let your mouth open and let out a big "HA" sound, as you chop the wood in one stroke.

Repeat this several times, as a group, inhaling and bringing the arms over the head, exhaling with a "HA" straight from the belly when the arms descend and pelvis lowers, still grounded into the earth, to chop the wood.

You can use other creative movement explorations of pushing the air away with arms, hands, legs and feet, pulling, wringing while shifting weight from one foot to the other forward, backward and sideways and diagonally, still feeling connected through the pelvis.

APPROACHING BALANCE MENTALLY: STILLING THE MIND
– Ages 8 and up

Emptying the mind, through the process of finding a stillness within, creates a profound inner balance. Stilling the mind brings about a readiness to listen to the truth within. All of us need to be able to attend to silence, in order to know ourselves.

Mental balance is directly connected to the breath. Breath is the life force, the great flow of energy, aligning mind and body with the flow of the universe.

SMOOTH BREATHING

Ask children to lie down quietly on the floor, on their backs, with their knees up and feet flat on the floor. Have them put their hands on their bellies and close their eyes.

Each time you breathe in, you can fill your belly with air, so that it puffs out like a balloon (diaphragmatic breathing). Then, as you exhale your hands come back toward the floor as your belly empties.

Breathing in, fill the balloon up, feel your hands move away from your body. As you exhale, the belly shrinks, and your hands sink back to the center.

Breathing should never be forced or controlled. Allow children to breathe according to their own rhythm, without straining or forcing.

BREATH OF SPIRIT

After a time, you can imagine breathing to be smooth, easy and effortless. You can even imagine that you are not doing the breathing at all, but each time the breath comes in, to fill your belly, it is Spirit (God, Great Spirit, Nature…) breathing life into your whole entire body, filling up every cell in your body with energy. As you exhale everything easily relaxes.

Just enjoy the sensation of being filled with unlimited love as the breath of Spirit fills your body with deep peace.

APPROACHING BALANCE THROUGH THE EMOTIONS:
THE POWER OF TOUCH TO HEAL

Touch can be a powerful facilitator for calming emotions and restoring inner balance. Children need the reassurance of a caring, loving touch from parents.

Holding, hugging, rocking, gentle touch—these are ways the emotions can be soothed into harmony. Love, the great balancer, flows naturally from a quiet assurance of a caring touch. Inner order is restored.

FOOT RUB – Ages 6 and up

Sitting in a circle on the floor or on chairs works best. Children can remove shoes and socks. Have children cross legs so that one foot rests cradled in one hand.

Begin to knead the sole of your foot from the arch upward to the ball.

Gently hold the heel of the foot with one hand and gently squeeze the heel a few times.

Make a fist with one hand, and press the knuckles into the soles of the feet.

Curl the toes and squeeze, then relax.

Hold onto the leg of the foot you've been working on, under the knee, and shake the foot out. Rotate the ankles in a circle several times in one direction, then reverse.

When you're ready, switch to the other foot.

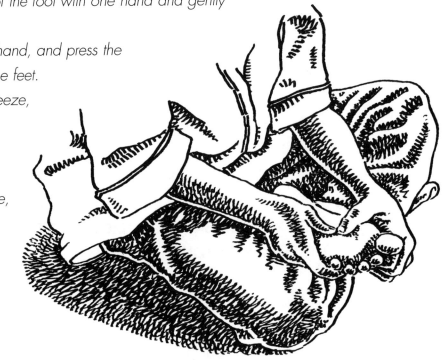

BACK-TO-BACK STRETCH

Group children into pairs, have them sit cross-legged, or with soles of the feet together, back-to-back. One person bends forward while the other person leans back, stretching out arms, and opening chest to the sky. Then have partners switch roles. Repeat very slowly several times.

SHOULDER RUB TRAIN

Standing together in a circle, each person reaches for the shoulders of the person ahead of them, and with their hands very gently squeezes and kneads the shoulders of that person to give a gentle massage.

Then the whole group turns around, and does the same with the person now standing in front of them.

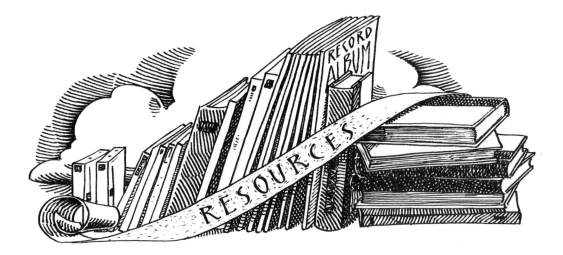

NINE: Developing Balance

Books for children:

Carr, Rachel. *Be a Frog, a Bird or a Tree: Rachel Carr's Creative Yoga Exercises for Children.* Illus. Don Hedin. New York: Harper & Row, 1977.

Music and songs:

✿ *indicates sound cassette or recording*
△ *indicates printed songbook collection*

✿ "I'm Gonna Reach." Pease, Tom. *I'm Gonna Reach.* Tomorrow River Music, 1989.

✿ "My Roots Go Down." Pirtle, Sarah. *Two Hands Hold The Earth.* A Gentle Wind, 1993.

✿ "With Two Wings." Grammer, Red. *Teaching Peace.* Smilin' Atcha Music, 1986.

Books for adults:

Benzwie, Teresa. *A Moving Experience: Dance for Lovers of Children and the Child Within.* Tucson: Zephyr Press, 1987.

Bonheim, Jalaja. *The Serpent and the Wave: A Guide to Movement Meditation.* Berkeley: Celestial Arts, 1992.

Developing Balance

Hendricks, Gay and Russel Wills. *The Centering Book: Awareness Activities for Children, Parents, and Teachers*. Englewood Cliffs, NJ: Prentice-Hall, 1989.

Huang, Chungliang A. *Embrace Tiger, Return to Mountain: The Essence of Tai Chi*. Reprinted ed. Berkeley: Celestial Arts, 1995.

Montagu, Ashley. *Touching: The Human Significance of the Skin*. New York: Columbia University Press, 1971.

Rush, Anne Kent. *The Back Rub Book*. New York: Vintage Books, 1989.

Speads, Carola H. *Breathing: The ABC's*. New York: Harper & Row, 1978.

Creating Joy

Let the voice sing out
in praise and thanksgiving.
Gather together in joyous song.
Celebrate the gift of Spirit.

From the earliest stages of social life, people have united in thanksgiving and song. The voice in praise is the instrument of the soul, carried by breath, the vital life force.

Song is harmony, and the practice of singing is the process of attuning the entire human instrument to universal energies from the earth and sky in balance and proportion.

Our earliest songs are oral poems, rhythms of humankind seeking to understand itself within the world. Words are indeed powerful tools. Words spoken in song can have the power to generate energy toward a beneficial goal, or contrarily, to speed the human experience into chaos.

When working with children, choose poems, rhythms and songs which express the fundamental connection to earth, the elements, the rhythms of life, the Divine Mystery.

Faith is strengthened by calling it forth in story and word, praises and thanksgiving. We show our children the strength of community, the power of compassion, the gifts of the spirit, through our shared songs and celebrations.

The voice is known as the instrument of the soul. In the following explorations, children are asked to use their natural voices to cultivate Self-expression, inner power and the freedom of making joyful noise.

SOUNDING THE NOTE

Begin by loosening up the body, shaking, stretching, then standing in a circle.

Inhale, and feel the belly fill up with air, exhale and let the air out with a big wide open mouth shaped into an "AAHHH" shape.

Let the sound continue until everyone has run out of breath, then repeat. Try doing it very, very quietly, and with a stronger force, gradually increase in volume.

Repeat until there is a nice flow of inhalation and exhalation/sounding.

NAME SONG

A child's name is her point of power, the quickening of her soul force in the world.

Start with having children sing their names any way they would like to. Then ask one person to sing at a time. The rest of the group responds by singing the name exactly as it was just sung. Continue going around the circle,

as a call-and-response until all the children have sung their name, and their name has been sung back to them. (Shy children may choose to whisper their name.)

NAME SONGS WITH MOVEMENT – Ages 6 and up

Let children spread out through the room, so each has enough space to move freely.

Allow children to begin by saying their name on their own. First very quietly, then slowly, then fast, high, low, shaky, loud, soft. Encourage children to move spontaneously as they sing these different name songs.

Have each child choose one way of saying or singing his name and repeat it that way, with movement/gesture added.

Return the group to a circle and have children, one at a time, repeat their name song with movement three times, as the group does it with them. Go around the circle until everyone has shared.

LISTEN TO THE SOUNDS OF LIFE

Create a quiet atmosphere in the room and ask children to pay attention to all the sounds they can hear. Let them listen quietly for at least three to five minutes.

Afterwards, have them share what they heard—inside sounds (breathing, someone scratching hair, chair moving, door opening) and outside sounds (a car passing, a plane, birds, rain, leaves blowing, people talking).

Create a soundscape by inviting children to volunteer making the sounds they heard.

HEARING SILENCE

Repeat the above listening exercise with the added task of having the children listen for the silence between sounds, for example, the silence between the notes of a bird's call.

Every time you are listening to sound, move your arm and hand; every time you are listening to silence, hold it still.

SING SONGS OF SPIRIT

Bring in instruments, or make your own, and start singing songs of Spirit. Here's a list to get you started, but use songs that best celebrate your own spiritual and cultural traditions.

Angels Watching Over You

Amazing Grace

'Tis a Gift To Be Simple

All God's Critters Got a Place in the Choir

Thanks a Lot

Where I Sit is Holy

Peace I Give

Day By Day

Dona Nobis

All the World is My Friend

Two Hands Hold The Earth

All I Really Need

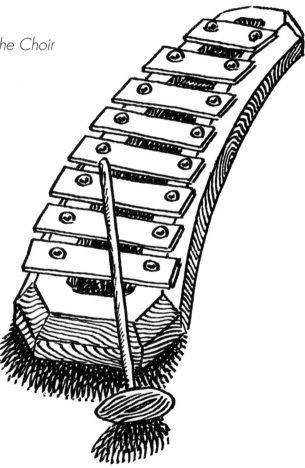

See Resources for recordings and music suggestions.

TEN: Creating Joy

Books with guided adventures in music for children:

DeBeer, Sara, ed. *Open Ears: Musical Adventures for a New Generation.* Rosyln, NY: Ellipsis Kids, 1995. *Writings by Allaudin & Devi Mathieu, Pete Seeger, David Darling, Paul McCartney, Phoebe Snow, Sally Rogers and many more.*

Hart, Avery and Paul Mantell. *Kids Make Music: Clapping & Tapping from Bach to Rock.* Illus. Loretta T. Braren. Charlotte, VT: Williamson Publishing, 1993.

Rhythm and poetry:

Fleischman, Paul. *I Am Phoenix: Poems for Two Voices.* Illus. Eric Beddows. New York: Harper & Row, 1985.

Fleischman, Paul. *Joyful Noise: Poems for Two Voices.* Illus. Eric Beddows. New York: Harper Trophy, 1992.

Larrick, Nancy. *Let's Do a Poem!* New York, Delacorte Press, 1991.

Kennedy, X. J. and Dorothy M. Kennedy, eds. *Talking Like the Rain: A First Book of Poems.* Illus. Jane Dyer. Boston: Little, Brown & Co, 1992.

Sullivan, Charles, ed. *Imaginary Gardens: American Poetry and Art for Young People.* New York: H.N. Abrams, 1989

Songbook collections:

Avni, Fran. *Jewish Songbooks for Children.* Tara Publications, 29 Derby Ave., Cedarhurst, NY 11516.

Blood, Peter and Annie Patterson, eds. *Rise Up Singing: The Group Singing Songbook.* Rev. ed. Bethlehem, PA: Sing-Out! Publications, 1992. *1200 songs including sections on "Sacred Rounds and Chants," "Gospel" and "Faith". Teaching tapes available.*

Children's Songs for A Friendly Planet. (Available through Michael Olaf's Essential Montessori catalogue, P.O. Box 1162, Arcata, CA 95521, (707) 826-1557.)

Gill, Madelaine, coll. and illus. *Praise for the Singing: Songs for Children.* Arranged by Greg Pliska. Boston: Little, Brown & Co, 1993. *African-American spirituals, American folksongs, church hymns, Shaker songs and Jewish songs.*

Jacobs, Rita. *Music for Young Children.* Stroud: Hawthorn, 1991.

Keoloha, Anne. *Songs of the Earth.* Berkeley, CA: Celestial Arts, 1989. *A collection of songs from African, Buddhist, Sufi, Jewish and other traditions.*

Krull, Kathleen, coll. *Songs of Praise.* Illus. Kathryn Hewitt. New York: Harcourt Brace Jovanovich, 1988. *Songs of praise in the Christian tradition.*

Metropolitan Museum of Art Staff. *Go In and Out the Window: An Illustrated Songbook for Young People.* New York: Metropolitan Museum of Art, 1987.

Simon, William L. and Dan Fox. *Reader's Digest Family Songbook of Faith and Joy: 129 All-Time Inspirational Favorites.* Pleasantville, NY: Reader's Digest Association, 1981.

Recorded music and songs for children:
many other artists are included in preceding Resources

Chapin, Tom. *Mother Earth*. Sony, 1990.

A Child's Celebration of Song. Music for Little People, 1992. *Musicians include James Taylor; Peter, Paul & Mary; Taj Mahal and many others.*

Earthrise: The Rainforest Album. Pyramid Records Group, 1994. *Various contemporary musicians such as Paul McCartney, Elton John and many others.*

Family Folk Festival. Music for Little People, 1990.

Fink, Cathy and Marcy Marxer. *A Cathy and Marcy Collection for Kids*. Rounder Records, 1994.

Golden Bough. *Kids at Heart*. Golden Bough/ARC Music U.S., 1993. *Music in Celtic tradition with children's voices, comes with lyrics and guitar chords.*

Grammer, Red. *Teaching Peace*. Smilin' Atcha Music, 1986.

Ladysmith Black Mambazo. *Gift of the Tortoise: A Musical Journey Through Southern Africa*. Music for Little People, 1994.

Los Lobos. *Papa's Dream*. Los Lobos with Lalo, Guerrero. Redway, CA: Music for Little People, 1995.

McCutcheon, John. *Family Garden*. Rounder Records, 1993.

Peace is the World Smiling. Music for Little People, 1989.

Pease, Tom. *I'm Gonna Reach*. Tomorrow River Music, 1993.

Penner, Fred. *A House for Me*. Oak Street Music, 1985.

Pirtle, Sarah. *Two Hands Hold the Earth*. A Gentle Wind, 1984.

Pirtle, Sarah. *Magical Earth*. A Gentle Wind, 1993.

Positively Reggae: An All Family Musical Celebration. Sony Wonder, 1994. *Messages of family, unity, peace and harmony.*

Raffi. *One Light One Sun, Baby Beluga, and Everything Grows*. MCA Records, 1985, 1977.

Raffi. *Evergreen, Everblue: An Ecology Album for the 90s*. MCA Records, 1990.

Rogers, Sally. *Piggyback Planet*. Round River Records, 1990.

Seeger Family. *Animal Folk Songs for Children*. Rounder Records, 1992.

Sweet Honey in the Rock. *I Got Shoes*. Music for Little People, 1994.

Tickle Tune Typhoon. *Healthy Beginnings*. Music for Little People, 1993.

Walters, J. Donald. *All the World is My Friend*. Education for Life Foundation, 1987.

Williamson, Robin. *Songs for Children of All Ages*. Flying Fish, 1987.

Recorded music of chants and of spirit songs for women and families:

Brooke Medicine Eagle. *A Gift of Song*. Harmony Network, P.O. Box 9725, Berkeley, CA 94709.

Libana. *A Circle is Cast: Rounds, Chants, and Songs for Celebration and Ritual*. Cambridge, MA: Spinning Record, 1986, and *Fire Within*, Durham, NC: Ladyslipper, 1990.

Songs of the Goddess. Sonoma County Birth Network, P.O. Box 1005, Occidental, CA 95465.

Zuleikha. *Heart Matters* and *White Pavilion: Songs with Zuleikha & Friends*. Zuleikha, P.O. Box 9139, Santa Fe, NM 87504.

Books for adults on the art of listening:

Inayat Khan, Hazrat. *The Music of Life.* New Lebanon, NY: Omega Press, 1988. *Topics such as harmony of life, the science of breath, the law of rhythm, creative process and the healing power of music and sound as told by a master musician and Sufi master.*

Mathieu, W. A. *The Listening Book: Discovering Your Own Music.* Boston: Shambhala Publications, 1991.

Mathieu, W. A. *The Musical Life: Reflections on What It Is and How to Live It.* Boston: Shambhala Publications, 1994.

Schafer, R. Murray. *The Tuning of The World.* New York: Alfred A. Knopf, 1977.

For children's music by mail order contact:

Alcazar.
P.O. Box 429, Waterbury, VT 05676, 800-541-9904.

Chinaberry.
2780 Via Orange Way, Suite B, Spring Valley, CA 91978, 800-776-2242.

Michael Olaf's Essential Montessori.
P.O. Box 1162, 1101 H Street, Arcata, CA 95521, 707-826-1557.

Music for Little People.
605 S. Douglas Street, El Segundo, CA 90245, 800-727-2233.

Afterword

It is my hope that this book has provided those who teach children practical support toward ensuring the blossoming of children's spiritual lives. If it is true that we teach what we most need to learn, then as teachers we need to remind ourselves that we will continue to learn these very same lessons of kindness, compassion, forgiveness, love and joy throughout our lives.

As guardians of these wise beings who are children, let us not assume we hold all the answers. What we can do as teachers is illuminate a moral path for those seeking a way to walk in balance through this spinning world.

> *Let us keep our hearts open*
> *To the joy of Unknowing,*
> *Our minds still in the presence*
> *Of Infinite Wisdom.*
> *Let us celebrate the Beloved*
> *In our caring love for one another.*

Send your stories and comments regarding implementing *Curriculum of Love* in your own work with children to: Grace Publishing & Communications, P.O. Box 6629, Charlottesville, VA 22906-6629.

Blessings to you and the children you serve.

- M.S.D.

GENERAL RESOURCES:

Books for adults on nurturing spirituality in children, conscious parenting and creative education:

Aronson, Linda. *Big Spirits, Little Bodies: Parenting Your Way to Wholeness*. Virginia Beach, VA: A.R.E. Press, 1995.

Baldwin, Rahima. *You Are Your Child's First Teacher*. Berkeley: Celestial Arts, 1989.

Berends, Polly Berrien. *Gently Lead: How to Teach Your Children about God While Finding Out for Yourself*. New York: Harper Collins, 1991.

Berends, Polly Berrien. *Whole Child/Whole Parent*. Rev. ed. New York: Harper & Row, 1983.

Coloroso, Barbara. *Kids Are Worth It! Giving Your Child the Gift of Inner Discipline*. New York: William Morrow, 1994.

Crary, Elizabeth. *Pick Up Your Socks – and Other Skills Growing Children Need*. Seattle: Parenting Press, 1990.

Dacey, John and Alex Packer. *The Nurturing Parent: How to Raise Creative, Loving, Responsible Children*. New York: Simon & Schuster, 1992.

Dietzel, Louise A. *Parenting with Respect and Peacefulness*. Lancaster, PA: Starburst Publishers, 1995.

Dosick, Wayne. *Golden Rules: The Ten Ethical Values Parents Need To Teach Their Children*. San Francisco: Harper San Francisco, 1995.

Dyer, Wayne. *What Do You Really Want For Your Children?* New York: Avon Books, 1985.

Elkind, David. *The Hurried Child: Growing Up Too Fast Too Soon.* Rev. ed. Reading, MA: Addison-Wesley Publishing, 1988.

Fields, Rick, ed. *Chop Wood, Carry Water: A Guide To Finding Spiritual Fulfillment in Everyday Life.* Los Angeles: J. P. Tarcher, 1984.

Fitzpatrick, Jean Grasso. *Small Wonder: How To Answer Your Child's Impossible Questions About Life.* New York: Viking, 1994.

Fitzpatrick, Jean Grasso. *Something More: Nurturing Your Child's Spiritual Growth.* New York: Viking, 1991.

Glenn, H. Stephen. *Raising Self-Reliant Children in a Self-Indulgent World: Seven Building Blocks for Developing Capable Young People.* Rocklin, CA: Prima Publishing & Communications, 1989.

Glennon, Will. *Fathering: Strengthening Connection with Your Children No Matter Where You Are.* Berkeley: Conari Press, 1995.

Hammond, Merryl and Rob Collins. *One World, One Earth: Educating Children for Social Responsibility.* Gabriola Island, B.C.: New Society Publishers, 1993.

Holt, John. *Learning All the Time.* Reading, MA: Addison-Wesley, 1989.

Hopkins, Susan and Jeffrey Winters, eds. *Discover the World: Empowering Children to Value Themselves, Others and The Earth.* Philadelphia: New Society Publishers, 1990.

Jenkins, Peggy. *The Joyful Child: A Sourcebook of Activities and Ideas for Releasing Children's Natural Joy.* Tucson: Harbinger House, 1989.

Kavelin-Popov, Linda and Dan Popov. *The Virtues Guide: A Handbook for Parents Teaching Virtues.* Rev. ed. Salt Spring Island, B.C.: The Virtues Project, 1993.

Kealoha, Anna. *Trust the Children: A Manual and Activity Guide for Homeschooling and Alternative Learning.* Berkeley: Celestial Arts, 1995.

Kilpatrick, William, Gregory Wolfe and Suzanne Wolfe. *Books That Build Character: A Guide to Teaching your Child Moral Values through Stories.* New York: Simon & Schuster, 1994.

Linthorst, Ann Tremaine. *Mothering As a Spiritual Journey: Learning to Let God Nurture Your Children and You Along With Them.* New York: Crossroad, 1993.

Orlick, Terry. *Free to Feel Great: Teaching Children to Excel at Living.* Carp, Ont.: Creative Bound, 1993.

Paris, Thomas and Eileen Paris. *I'll Never Do to my Kids what my Parents Did to Me! A Guide to Conscious Parenting.* New York: Warner Books, 1992.

Pearce, Joseph Chilton. *Evolution's End: Claiming the Potential of Our Intelligence.* San Francisco: Harper San Francisco, 1993.

Pearce, Joseph Chilton. *Magical Child: Rediscovering Nature's Plan for Our Children.* New York: Bantam Books, 1980.

Prather, Hugh and Gayle Prather. *Spiritual Parenting: A Guide to Understanding and Nurturing the Heart of Your Child.* Crown/Harmony, 1996.

Reuben, Steven Carr. *Raising Ethical Children: 10 Keys to Helping Your Children Become Moral and Caring.* Rocklin, CA: Prima, 1994.

Singh, Tara. *Awakening a Child from Within.* Los Angeles: Life Action Press, 1991.

Singh, Tara. *How to Raise a Child of God.* Los Angeles: Life Action Press, 1987.

Thomson, John, ed. *Natural Childhood.* New York: Simon & Schuster, 1994. *A Rudolf Steiner based philosophy on raising children.*

Vissel, Barry and Joyce Vissel. *Models of Love: The Parent-Child Journey.* Aptos, CA: Ramira Publishing, 1986.

Walters, J. Donald. *Education for Life.* Nevada City, CA: Ananda Publications, 1986.

Illustrated books for children on the nature of God:

Boritzer, Etan. *What is God?* Willowdale, Ont.: Firefly, 1990.

Carlstrom, Nancy White. *Does God Know How to Tie Shoes?* Illus. Lori McElrath-Eslick. Grand Rapids, MI: William B. Eerdmans, 1993.

Kroll, Virginia. *I Want to Know All About God.* Illus. Debra Reid Jenkins. Grand Rapids, MI: William B. Eerdmans Publishing, 1994. *Children wonder about and discover God in their everyday experiences.*

Meehan, Bridget Mary and Regina Madonna Oliver. *Heart Talks with Mother God.* Illus. Susan K. Sawyer. Collegeville, MN: Liturgical Press, 1995. *Stories and paintings to help children experience the feminine face of God as reflected in Scripture.*

Sasso, Sandy E. *But God Remembered: Stories of Women from Creation to the Promised Land.* Illus. Bethanne Andersen. Woodstock, VT: Jewish Lights Publishing, 1995.

Sasso, Sandy E. *God's Paintbrush.* Illus. Annette C. Compton. Woodstock, VT: Jewish Lights Publishing, 1992.

Sasso, Sandy E. *In God's Name.* Illus. Phoebe Stone. Woodstock, VT: Jewish Lights Publishing, 1994. *A nondenominational, nonsectarian celebration of people of the world and their belief in God.*

Snyder, Carol. *God Must Like Cookies, Too.* Illus. Beth Glick. Philadelphia: Jewish Publication Society, 1993.

Williamson, Marianne. *Emma and Mommy Talk to God.* New York: Harper Collins, 1996.

Books for adults on the nature of God:

Anderson, Sherry Ruth and Patricia Hopkins. *The Feminine Face of God: The Unfolding of the Sacred in Women.* New York: Bantam Books, 1991.

Armstrong, Karen. *History of God: The 4000-Year Quest of Judaism, Christianity, and Islam.* New York: Ballantine Books, 1994.

Gellman, Marc. *How Do You Spell God? Answers to the Big Questions from Around the World.* Illus. Joseph A. Smith. New York: Morrow Junior Books, 1995.

Gellman, Marc and Thomas Hartman. *Where Does God Live?* New York: Triumph Books, 1991.

Kushner, Harold. *When Children Ask About God.* Rev. ed. New York: Schocken Books, 1989.

Talking To Your Children About God: A Book For Families of All Faiths. Berkeley, CA: Berkeley Publishers, 1994.

More illustrated books for children:

Bennett, William, ed. *The Children's Book of Virtues.* Illus. Michael Hague. New York: Simon & Schuster, 1995.

Doe, Mimi and Garland Waller. *Drawing Angels Near.* New York: Pocket Books, 1995. *Children Tell of Angels in Words and Pictures.*

Fox, Matthew. *In the Beginning There Was Joy: A Celebration of Creation for Children of all Ages.* Illus. Jane Tattersfield. New York: Crossroad, 1995. *A celebration of creation as a gift of hope, wonder and joy.*

Gerstein, Mordicai. *The Shadow of a Flying Bird: A Legend from the Kurdistani Jews.* New York: Hyperion Books for Children, 1994.

Grifalconi, Ann. *The Bravest Flute: A Story of Courage in the Mayan Tradition*. Boston: Little, Brown & Co., 1994.

Hastings, Selina. *The Children's Illustrated Bible*. Illus. Eric Thomas and Amy Burch. New York: Dorling Kindersley, 1994.

Hodges, Margaret. *Brother Francis and the Friendly Beasts*. Illus. Ted Lewin. New York: Scribner, 1991.

Johnson, James Weldon. *The Creation*. Ed. James Ransome. New York: Holiday House, 1994. *An African-American retelling of the Creation story.*

Payne, Lauren M. *Just Because I Am: A Child's Book of Affirmation*. Illus. Claudia Rohling. Minneapolis: Free Spirit Publishing, 1994.

Wood, Douglas. *Old Turtle*. Illus. Cheng-Khee Chee. Duluth, MN: Pfeifer Hamilton, 1992.

Books for older children to adult:

Bennett, William, ed. *The Book of Virtues: A Treasury of Great Moral Stories*. New York: Simon & Schuster, 1993.

Bennett, William, ed. *The Moral Compass: Stories for a Life's Journey*. New York: Simon & Schuster, 1995.

Boone, J. Allen. *Kinship With All Life*. New York: Harper & Row, 1976.

Canfield, Jack and Mark Victor Hansen, eds. *Chicken Soup for the Soul: 101 Stories to Open the Heart and Rekindle the Spirit*. Deerfield Beach, FL: Health Communications, 1993.

Canfield, Jack and Mark Victor Hansen, eds. *A Second Helping: 101 More Stories to Open the Heart and Rekindle the Spirit*. Deerfield Beach, FL: Health Communications, 1995.

Carter, Forrest. *The Education of Little Tree*. New York: Delacorte Press, 1976.

Lewis, C. S. *Chronicles of Narnia*. New York: Harper Trophy, 1984.

Summer Rain, Mary. *Mountains, Meadows and Moonbeams: A Child's Spiritual Reader.* Norfolk, VA: Hampton Roads Publishing Co., 1984.

More books of spirit for adults:

Edelman, Marian Wright. *Guide My Feet: Prayers and Meditations on Loving and Working for Children*. Boston: Beacon Press, 1995.

Grabowsky, Mary Ford, comp. *Prayers for All People*. New York: Doubleday, 1995.

Jalal al-Din Rumi, Maulana. *The Essential Rumi*. Trans. Coleman Barks. San Francisco: Harper San Francisco, 1995.

Krishnamurti, J. *The Book of Life. Daily Meditations with J. Krishnamurti*. San Francisco: Harper San Francisco, 1995.

Williamson, Marianne. *Illuminata: A Return to Prayer*. New York: Riverhead Books, 1994.

Companies providing mail-order resources:

Animal Town, cooperative games, toys, books
P.O. Box 485, Healdsburg, CA 95448, 800-445-8642.

August House Publishers, storytelling, books, tapes
P.O. Box 381316, Little Rock, AK 72203, 501-372-5450.

Caedmon Records/Harper Audio
12 E. 53rd Street, New York, NY 10022, 212-207-7000.

Chinaberry, books, tapes, and treasures
2780 Via Orange Way, Suite B, Spring Valley, CA 91978, 800-776-2242.

HearthSong, toys, crafts, books
156 N. Main St., Sebastopol, CA 95472, 800-325-2502.

Michael Olaf's Essential Montessori, books, toys, tapes and resources for homes and schools
P.O. Box 1162, 1101 H Street, Arcata, CA 95521, 707-826-1557.

Music for Little People, music, videos, instruments, games
605 S. Douglas Street, El Segundo, CA 90245, 800-727-2233.

National Storytelling Association
P.O. Box 309, Jonesborough, TN 37659-0309, 423-753-2171.

The Heritage Key, An International Children's Catalogue, multi-cultural books, toys and dolls
6102 E. Mescal, Scottsdale, AZ 85254, 602-483-3313.

Whole Child, books for gentle parenting, activities for creative play
P.O. Box 100, Campbellville, ON, Canada L0P 1B0, 800-387-2888.

Wonder of Words, books and games
9520 Padgett St. Suite 212, San Diego, CA 92126.

Yellow Moon Press, storytelling tapes
P.O. Box 38136, Cambridge, MA 02238, 800-497-4385.

About the Author

Morgan Simone Daleo is a mother, educator, writer and performing artist who has been teaching, performing and working with both children and adults through the creative arts for more than twenty years.

A former Artist-in-the-Schools through the N.Y. State Council for the Arts, she has also taught on the Theatre Arts faculties of Sonoma State University, and Wesleyan University. She holds a B.A. degree from Trinity College and a M.A. in Liberal Studies from Wesleyan University where she focused on Movement as a Healing Art.

Trained extensively in both dance and theater, Morgan's storytelling performances which blend movement, song, stories and improvisation, have entertained audiences of all ages at schools, libraries and festivals throughout the United States and abroad. Her background has also proved useful in the creative task of homeschooling and amusing her children.

Morgan lives in Charlottesville, Virginia with her husband, artist/illustrator Frank Riccio, two spirited children and a cat who likes to roam.

Index

Activities are listed as subentries under the main entry subject heading of occurence, e.g., "crayon rubbings" will be found under "Beauty."

NEW BOOKS

THE BOOK OF DREAMS & VISIONS

A Journal Guide for Working with Night Dreams and Day Dreams

with an introduction by Morgan Simone Daleo

Dreams are a gateway to the creative imagination. This book offers dreamers, ages 10 through adult, simple and practical suggestions on how to use their own night dreams and day dreams or inner visions for greater self-understanding, inspiration and to help achieve personal goals.

Provides space for writing and drawing one's own dreams and visions.

8 1/2"x 5 1/2", 120 pages, spiral bound includes blank & lined pages with border illustrations, ISBN 0-9648799-6-4, $15.00 (Dreamwork/Creativity)

Forthcoming:

A SPIRITED ALPHABET

Morgan Simone Daleo
Illustrated by Frank Riccio

"A is for angel asleep in his bed, B for the beauty of birds over-head..." So begins this lovely alphabet primer, blending lilting rhyme with tender illustrations to celebrate the wonders of a child's world and the mysteries of nature. Award-winning artist, Frank Riccio captures a joyful spirit of delight as children learn to honor values such as faith, love, trust and unity.

6"x 9" Hardcover 32 illustrated pages
ISBN 0-9648799-5-6 (All ages)
Publication date: December 1996

ORDER FORM

Grace Publishing & Communications
P.O. Box 6629 • Charlottesville, VA 22906-6629

Please send me your free catalogue/newsletter celebrating creativity and spirit in children and families.

Name _____

Address _____

City _____ State _____ Zip _____

Phone (   ) _____

I would like to order the following:

QTY	TITLE / ITEM	PRICE EACH	PRICE
	Curriculum of Love	$17.95	
	Subtotal		
	Sales Tax (Virginia Residents)		
	Shipping (see below)		
	Total Enclosed		

Make checks payable to: **Grace Publishing & Communications**

SHIPPING RATES: Postal book rate: $2.50 first book; $1.00 each additional
Air mail or Priority: $3.50 per book